ENDORSEMENTS

Sex is everywhere. It's on our phones, on our tablets, and on our minds. We hear about how everyone is having it more than us, everyone is enjoying it more than us, and everyone is more satisfied than us. But if that is true, why are counseling offices filled with people trying to piece their lives back together after a relationship filled with sexual freedom and fulfilling fantasies ended and left them devastated? Why is Gen Z finding its easier to be alone with porn than it is to be with another person? It seems we've thrown out the instructions and created a disaster. What would it look like for a mother of four and a follower of Jesus and a happy wife for over 30 years to give some insight into this? That's what this book is about. It's for every young reader to find hope and every broken heart to find healing.

RUSTY GEORGE
Lead Pastor, Real Life Church
reallifechurch.org
pastorrustygeorge.com

Let's just be honest: sex feels really good. It was designed to feel good. God created us with pleasure spots. There's no other conclusion than God wants us to fully enjoy the act of physical unity. But this pleasure comes with a seemingly oppressive and behind-the-times caveat: wait until you're married. Why would God restrict such a wonderful gift to the tightest of guidelines? A question for the ages.

We're bullied until we do and shamed when we have. The real problem? "Should I, or should I not, have sex?," is the wrong question.

I'm convinced God's caveat is his protection of who we are. Why does God want to protect me—my heart, my soul, my character, my identity—in this way? What is so important about my spirit that God would design my body for pleasure and then ask me to wait for years to enjoy it? What's the big deal? These are the questions to ask. Chana does a fine job of answering them.

TARA HOKE SCHIRO
MA, Author, Cohost of *Two Steps Ahead* Podcast:
Highlighting the Shit We've Stepped in So You Don't Have To

I've worked with students for the last 12 years, first with Millennials and now Gen Z'ers. And one trend has remained: the "normal way" of dating and sex is broken and leaves people broken. We need "sexual mavericks." Chana writes in a real and refreshing way that doesn't pull any punches and yet keeps love and sincerity always at the forefront. This book is for anyone looking for real love, sex, and intimacy that will last for a lifetime, never get old, and always be fulfilling.

MATT DENTON
Student Ministry Director, Real Life Church
yxyouth.com

Chana's book is a breath of fresh air! There is no condemnation for someone who's been (or still is) like I was; a victim of child molestation who lost my sense of self-worth. There is no guilt or shame rolling off these pages. There's an invitation. An invitation to a paradigm shift to think about sex differently, even when everyone is trying to sell you a cheap imitation.

So turn the page, not with dread, but excitement to explore God's purpose for and joy in the most intimate of human relationships!

SARAH J.R. SMITH
YA author who writes under the pseudonym "Precarious Yates"
Precariousyates.com

I met Chana Keefer when we were both trying (with different organizations) to counter the sex-saturated perspective being taught in public schools. We saw rising sexually transmitted infections, damaged self-images, a declining interest in marriage, and an increase in divorce. And we saw young people who were desperate for a map to avoid those pitfalls.

Chana's passion came across and left a lasting impact on her audience. She has a heart to point young people toward the highest possible standard, the Olympic Gold of relationships. The one God Himself designed for them to enjoy. She knows how hard it is to get there, because she navigated it herself—not perfectly or without a few close calls—but she found her *Great Love for Life* because she absorbed the wisdom of those who had gone before her. Now she wants to pass along the wisdom she received to anyone who has the same desire for Olympic Gold in their relationship.

If you are, or you know, a teen or young adult who is facing ridicule, loneliness, and ostracism as they lean into God's plan, I highly recommend you get this book into their hands.

KAREN KROPF
Author, Speaker
Founder and Director Positively Waiting! Inc.

One day, I asked my high-school-age daughter what she thought was the most helpful part of my parenting. She quickly answered, "Being real." The fact that I'd been honest about the thoughts, actions, and insecurities I'd had traveling the road she travels today. She is keenly aware of both the good and bad choices I made, as well as the ramifications of each.

That's what I love about Chana Keefer's book, *Great Love for Life*. It's real, genuine, authentic! It draws pictures from true life experiences with engaging clarity.

I wish I had a book like this when I was wading through the choppy waters of dating! One that did not talk down to me or hide the realities of what I had to face. One that allowed me to see the fruits of godly choices and prepared me for the myriad of distractions and roadblocks along the way.

That is what *being real* with my daughter meant to her. It is also what Chana's straight talk about choosing a great love for life will be for you. I'd recommend parents, youth leaders, and teens use this book to start a much-needed conversation. And if you are one of those teens and the adults in your life haven't *gone there* with you yet, read the book yourself, take the ideas to Jesus in prayer and ask Him to imprint them on your soul. You will be grateful on your wedding night and each successive night of your marriage afterward.

CONNIE ALMONY
Licensed Therapist, Author
ConnieAlmony.com

As a father of two pre-teen girls, *Great Love for Life* is not only timely but a fantastic blueprint. Filled with anecdotal stories, encouragement and grounded advice, Chana has crafted a powerful argument against the "instant gratification" culture that permeates modern conversations about sex.

CHRIS DOWLING
Screenwriter, Director: *Run the Race & Where Hope Grows*
IMDB Link

My heartfelt appreciation goes out to Chana Keefer for tackling the subject of sexual purity, a timely and delicate issue in today's cultural climate. In our own embarrassment or fear of judgment, we often find ourselves skirting awkwardly around matters such as *sexual preference* and *how far is too far?*, and avoiding altogether the lightly trod ground of *abstinence* and *monogamy*.

In this author's able hands, the topic of sex, and God's ideas on the matter, are handled carefully, respectfully and truthfully. It is with this open heart that she offers personal testimony and practical advice that will pave the way for necessary discussion, that if applied, can help even those who have already delved into the world of sex to find their way back to a life of wholeness before God. I can't think of a more caring, thoughtful book on the subject, nor of a more talented and well-equipped writer to deliver it.

DANA PRATOLA
Author of the *Descended* series
DanaPratolaRomance.com

I spent nearly half of my adult life addicted to pornography.

This secret obsession took me down a road that eventually cost me everything. On the outside, everything in my life appeared to be wonderful. I was a pastor, celebrated conference speaker and best-selling author. I had been married 30 years, blessed with three sons and living our dream life in the white-collar suburb of Frisco, Texas.

Easter 2010, it was all gone in 24 hours.

My secret life of lust and sexual vice was a front-page story in *The Dallas Morning News*. Within twelve months, my marriage was gone, my career up in smoke and I was completely bankrupt. It has taken me ten formidable years to unearth a resurrected life. Today, God graciously uses my journey to freedom to equip other men and help them avoid the culmination of unchecked lust—death. The writer of Proverbs warns us of this ending...

> *"Many are the victims she has brought down; her slain are a mighty throng. Her house is a highway to the grave, leading down to the chambers of death." Proverbs 7:26-27*

Let me be clear here. The use of a female as the enticer in this chapter should not be misunderstood. This is both a male and female issue. Women are not the problem. Men are not the problem. Our *own* lust and sin—are the problem.

Which brings me to the reason I am so honored and happy to write this foreword.

Chana Keefer and her husband Mark have been beloved friends of mine for a couple decades. Together they have faithfully navigated the turbulent waters of marriage and raising a family in our modern culture. And they have done it well!

The words, chapters and story of *Great Love for Life* are powerful and truly will be life altering for the reader. But I do want you to understand who these words are coming from. Chana and Mark write out of a wealth of wise and impassioned living, marked by a brave love for the world they live in. You will feel their heart coming off each page.

Read slowly and carefully. Allow the revelation that comes from each chapter to inspire you. Perhaps even save you.

You will certainly uncover the painful traps of misusing sex in our current culture, but much more essential than that, you will reimagine God's ultimate intention for the gift of sexuality in the lives of the people He loves.

Enough. Let's read!

BLAINE BARTEL
Speaker, Recovery Coach & Bestselling Author of
*Death by a Thousand Lies: My Cover Up,
My Crash & My Resurrection From Sexual Addiction*
BlaineBartel.com

GREAT LOVE FOR LIFE

HOW TO FIND & KEEP LOVE THAT TRULY SATISFIES

CHANA KEEFER

old barn press

Great Love for Life
How to Find & Keep Love That Truly Satisfies
By Chana Keefer

Copyright© 2020 Chana Keefer. All rights reserved. Except for brief quotations for review purposes, no part of this book may be reproduced in any form without prior written permission from the author.

Cover design and interior layout | Yvonne Parks | PearCreative.ca

ISBN (Print): 978-0-9892197-9-2
ISBN (Ebook): 978-1-7361481-0-5

DEDICATION

This book is dedicated to Marty Walker, the adorable, gutsy camp counselor who ignored my immature giggles and shared life-saving, love-preserving advice when I needed it the most—BEFORE I thought I needed it!

Marty is in Heaven now, but her legacy lives on in me and in the countless lives she touched.

CONTENTS

Foreword	1
CHAPTER 1 | A Hot Mess	3
CHAPTER 2 | Lookin' For Love	11
CHAPTER 3 | The Disease	17
CHAPTER 4 | The Sexual Epidemic	23
CHAPTER 5 | Sweet Poison	29
CHAPTER 6 | The Sexual Avalanche	35
CHAPTER 7 | One Choice/Infinite Consequences	41
CHAPTER 8 | What's Pushing You To "Just Do It?"	49
CHAPTER 9 | The Enemy Within	57
CHAPTER 10 | Deadly Sexual Stumbling Blocks	69
CHAPTER 11 | Believing the Impossible	79
CHAPTER 12 | The Waiting Game	85
CHAPTER 13 | The Goal	91
CHAPTER 14 | Sexternal Pressures	99
CHAPTER 15 | On Modesty	107
CHAPTER 16 | A Purpose-FULL Lifestyle	115
CHAPTER 17 | How NOT To Go There—(Sexual Preservation 101)	121

CHAPTER 18	Avoid the "Sexual Rapids"	129
CHAPTER 19	The Voices in Your Head	135
CHAPTER 20	True Love Exercises Self-Control	145
CHAPTER 21	Who's On First?	153
CHAPTER 22	Laying a Foundation	159
CHAPTER 23	I Screwed Up. Now What?	169
CHAPTER 24	What If You Had No Choice?	181
CHAPTER 25	Stay Alert!	191
CHAPTER 26	On Shackin' Up	195
CHAPTER 27	Boys To Men	205
CHAPTER 28	Single and Intimate	213
CHAPTER 29	Dear Parents	219
CHAPTER 30	Quick Reference Guide:	231

Recommended Resources   233

Acknowledgements   235

FOREWORD

God is pro-sex. Have you ever heard that before? Many people harbor the notion that God is somehow anti-sex, especially people who don't know God up close and personal. When you know God, *really know God*, you discover He's a big fan of sex. In a recent interview for a conference on intimacy, I was asked, "Don't Christians believe God says sex is only for makin' babies?"

I laughed out loud.

My answer, "No, not at all."

Have you ever believed that myth? If so, read through Song of Songs and you'll find evidence to dismantle that falsehood. Physical intimacy is great and wonderful and magical. God made it this way—magnificent beyond all imagination.

Sadly, we run into a big problem when we follow our own roadmap to intimacy instead of God's master plan. I get it, no one likes to wait. I know I don't, but sometimes God asks us to do things that don't make sense to us *for our good*.

God created sex for us to enjoy—our anatomy points to this—and the best way to enjoy this gift is God's way.

But what is God's way?

This is what *Great Love for Life* is all about. This book you are holding in your hands is your escort to lasting love—with the Bible as your guide. Allow Chana to navigate you through the process of finding your true love. You'll discover what to look for in a spouse as you listen for God, protect your heart, wait on God, prepare yourself for your future, and secure the kind of love only God can give.

I truly believe if the biblical foundations presented here in *Great Love for Life* were followed, there would be fewer divorces, happier marriages, and more fulfilling sex lives.

Are you ready to discover *how to find and keep love that truly satisfies*? Keep reading. You'll be glad you did, and so will your future spouse.

LUCILLE WILLIAMS
Bestselling Author of *From Me to We* and
The Intimacy You Crave: Straight Talk About Sex And Pancakes
LuSays.com

CHAPTER 1

A HOT MESS

"I'm goin' nowhere. Somebody help me."
THE BEE GEES - *STAYIN' ALIVE*

My best friend and I giggle as we enter the room with the scotch-taped sign by the door that reads "Sex, Love and Dating." There are only girls in the room. Good. Slightly less embarrassing. I look down at my flat chest, scrawny legs poking from my favorite red shorts and follow the sunburned, mosquito-bitten appendages until they end in feet that look twice as long as they have any right to be. No danger I will have to deal with the subject of dating any time soon—if ever. But my friend? She is way ahead of me. All dimples, giggles, soft brown curls, blossoming body and baby blue eyes that turn every guy's head. She even has a steady boyfriend. I can't even imagine.

I don't know what I expect our teacher for this class to be like; perhaps a mousy woman with a monotone voice who holds up graphs and quotes statistics. But the woman named Marty with the bright red hair, glowing smile, and teasing twinkle in her eye is a definite surprise. She has an unashamed, refreshing way of speaking to us in her gorgeous southern drawl as peers—not as kids who need a lecture. Her infectious laugh and disarming way of looking each of us in the eye as she speaks make me feel truly seen rather than overlooked.

Marty doesn't hold back on how tough it was to navigate public school with high standards. She tells of ridicule from friends who would give her a hard time for choosing to not have sex; cute guys who would not ask her out because they knew she was "different"; crass jokes that would stop just because she walked in the room. "But when it came time to choose a Homecoming Queen," Marty pauses, "who do you think they chose?" She points a thumb toward herself.

And there was someone else who noticed Marty didn't fit in. Marty's oh-so-handsome future husband Mike noticed how she stood out from the crowd, respecting herself enough to earn the respect of others.

Her exact words are not what gets to my heart. It is the way her eyes glow when she refers to their wedding night and what a joy it was to discover sex for the first time, together, because they both were virgins. (All in a very G-rated manner that makes me blush nonetheless.)

In one short hour, Marty opens my eyes and changes the trajectory of my life. From this moment on, waiting for sex until my Honeymoon is my goal.

> As a kid you hear about it (sex) in the context of being wrong, being naughty. You don't think about it being something God created. I think sex gets a bad rap early on because it's misunderstood.
> **WONDER-HUBBY MARK**

In Jr. High, I was no wiser than the next twelve-year-old. I knew just enough about love and sex to be dangerous. It was all about how some guy would make me feel, how he would look, how the world would just *stop* when HE looked in my eyes. I admit, the rumors I'd heard about how sex really works grossed me out—but I didn't focus on that. If I had had the opportunity at twelve and thirteen to experiment sexually, God help me. I was so insecure and looking to other people for validation, I would have done something stupid. I just know it.

Luckily, I met some heroes who gave me priceless tips to help me make it to my wedding night relatively unscathed.

Throughout *Great Love for Life*, I will introduce you to heroes from all walks of life who have come to believe in healthy monogamy. You'll meet a victim of child abuse, a former Saturday Night Live comedienne, a woman who has spoken to thousands of high school students, telling her story of heartbreak and redemption, even a physical therapist who treats victims of horrific, violent sexual abuse. And many more.

Every story is different, but all are willing to bare their souls to help you have the kind of joyful love relationship you were created for.

That's my goal in *Great Love for Life*—to pass on information that will steer you away from the cliff of sexual disaster, a cliff I too was headed for.

The heartbreak of today's push toward casual sex is that we all long for intimacy. My husband and I have a great marriage that began with a mutual decision to uphold each other's virginity until our wedding night. No, life is not always a bowl of cherries and there is *much* more involved with a great marriage besides awesome sex, but sex is a key factor where so many are shooting themselves in the foot before "I Do" is ever exchanged.

Perhaps you shot yourself in both feet long ago. There's no judgment here. Just a message of hope and redemption. No one is pure as the driven snow and sometimes "hopeless" is the best place to get a fresh start.

YOU are priceless. No matter what you've done or where you've been, God accepts you, loves you with mind-blowing intensity, and has GOOD PLANS in mind for your future. Where you're weak, He can make you strong.

Virgin or not, God is GREAT at making beauty from ashes.

ALIVE: a.live (adj.)—living, lively, thriving.

Many people, by the time they enter into what is supposed to be a committed, legal, lifetime relationship, are no longer sexually *alive*. Somewhere along the way, sex and love has lost its zest and meaning. Rather than an experience of wonder, mystery, and beauty, sex has become enmeshed with the lowest instincts and weaknesses—a thing of shame to hide or even fear.

THAT IS NOT WHAT SEX IS SUPPOSED TO BE!!

Did I shout that loud enough?

THAT IS NOT WHAT SEX IS SUPPOSED TO BE!!

Sex, when protected and treasured until it's shared with the right person in a committed, lifetime, legal relationship, retains its "living, lively, thriving" nature. Sex in its purest form is a beautiful, mysterious, healing, bonding, and *holy* experience.

Plain and simple, I want **you** to experience sex and love as it was meant to be—vital, thriving, fun, and as unique as your fingerprint *times infinity*—because it's the melding of two unique personalities with endless facets into one, complex *whole*.

Sexual fulfillment today has been stolen from us with the lie of free and easy sex. We laughingly pour out our intimacy and ability to trust, then blink in bewilderment when we realize the cup is empty. But when we protect that cup, the two becoming one keeps our cup overflowing for a lifetime.

Have you ever heard of Russian Roulette? It's a terribly dangerous game using a gun with just one bullet. The only way to "win" at Russian Roulette is for the other person to die. The game of dating the way many people play it these days seems as dangerous and foolish as Russian Roulette. The more we "pull the trigger" to be sexually intimate without a lifetime commitment, the higher our chances are of contracting sexually transmitted diseases or making an unplanned baby. Beyond the physical ramifications, we exit each risky sexual interaction with a scarred heart and more roadblocks to the lifetime of lovingly intimate sexual fulfillment we desire.

Hopefully, the information in this book can help you decide that Sexual Russian Roulette is a game you will choose to avoid.

And what's my motivation for sticking my nose into your private choices? Basically, I care, and I couldn't sit on the sidelines any longer watching young people rob themselves blind of relational fulfillment. I felt I was witnessing a mugging without lifting a finger to intervene. Sure, there are fine individuals and groups out there speaking about sexual topics, but they're sorely outnumbered and young people right and left are dying, getting abortions, or wishing they were dead due to believing the lies of casual sex.

To sit by and do nothing? Nope. Time to fight.

Besides, I shudder to think what my life would have been if some gutsy camp counselors had decided it was someone else's job to get honest and speak out about sex.

Great Love for Life is here because *God loves you* enough to motivate lazy me to write it. His passion for you is the driving force.

By the way, that's the *real* intimacy the devil is killing when he convinces you to get sexually active outside of a legal, life-long, loving relationship.

The exciting news is, regardless of where you are now—from optimistic virgin to sexual veteran and all points in between—intimacy with God is what your heart craves.

In the grand scheme of things, I'm nothing. (How's that for a glowing list of accolades?) But I do happen to have a *vital, thriving, alive* relationship with the One who made you and me. Your Maker is the One who will *always* be there, *always* has your best in mind, *always* knows what's right, *always* loves no matter what, and is the *only* One big enough to fill the black hole in your heart.

He's the One who created the gift of sex in the first place. It just makes sense that the Master Craftsman would know how sex works best. I'm here to attest to the fact that…YES—HE DOES!

CHAPTER 2

LOOKIN' FOR LOVE

"True love never can be rent
but only true love can keep beauty innocent."
U2 - *A MAN AND A WOMAN*

THE CONTRACT: CIRCA 1938

Johnny Talent walked into Secretary Sarah's office and slumped into a chair, eyes wide and troubled, shoulders slumped in defeat, obviously carrying worries on his shoulders that were far beyond his years and experience.

"What's wrong?" Sarah asked, though she knew what was troubling him.

Johnny had what, in Hollywood, was known as "the goods." He was handsome, talented beyond reason, and had a natural charisma that transferred seamlessly to the big screen. An obvious star ready to launch into the big time. What was troubling him was an all-too-familiar scenario.

"I got offered the part," he stated, though his tone was that of one just sentenced to death by firing squad.

"And?" Sarah prompted. Her stomach churned with anger, knowing what he had just endured.

"I guess I should be grateful, I mean, they are taking a chance by casting an unknown."

Sarah slammed her desk drawer shut with undue force and took a deep breath. Her hands shook with suppressed rage as she crossed the room, glanced up and down the hall and quietly closed the door to her office. "Let me see it," she said, reaching for the papers Johnny held in his hands. Sarah returned to her chair and skimmed the document. Yep. Same as always.

The numbers on the page were insultingly low. The agreement he was to sign was completely one-sided, ensuring the movie-making mogul would make out like a bandit while this hard-working young man would get peanuts for his natural gifting and years of training, not to mention sacrifice, that had prepared him for this moment.

Sarah's boss, Mr. Big Shot, who had inherited the movie studio through his father and grandfather, had perfected this power move. Johnny was exactly what Big Shot looked for; gifted and valuable and poised on the brink of success but separated from all that was familiar, hundreds of miles away from family and friends who believed in him. Johnny had left all that behind to pursue his passion. Now he was swimming with sharks, like

Big Shot, who had no qualms about bleeding young talent dry for their own gain.

"He told you he had several other young actors dying to play this role, right?"

Johnny nodded.

"He said you were over-confident and your acting ability was 'raw,' right?"

Without a word, he nodded again.

"He said if you turned down this offer, he would make sure you never worked in 'his town,' again." Sarah's voice dripped with sarcasm.

Sarah had tried to keep quiet for months. She had watched, heartbroken, as so many talented young men and women had stumbled out of Big Shot's office with the same stricken expression, their crushed hopes and dreams trailing behind them as if he had disemboweled their future. She couldn't stand by and watch the carnage any longer.

"He's lying to you," Sarah stated.

Johnny's eyes shot up to hers.

"Big Shot knows other movie studios are interested in you; other huge projects are right around the corner. But, if you sign this contract, he has you. He will pay you peanuts for a role that deserves A-list pay and he will make sure to talk you down, steal your confidence, even steal the joy of doing work you love until you no longer believe in yourself and think chicken feed is what you deserve."

Johnny's mouth hung open. He took a deep breath. "Why are you telling me this?"

"Because I feel like a rat for not speaking up before. Big Shot is an evil spider who gets a kick out of sucking away the life of people who have incredible potential. He's a user. A shark. A vampire. Young, gifted actors like you are his favorite feast."

Johnny leaned forward, contract in his hand.

Sarah pulled out a list containing scale pay for acting in major motion pictures. She pointed to the lowest tier. "This is what he has applied to your contract. But this," she pointed three tiers up, "is what those numbers should be; what you deserve."

Johnny gasped.

"Not only that," Sarah pointed to several of the clauses in the contract, "He should be providing a place to live, a generous food allowance, assured days off, guaranteed pay for sickness, basically so many perks that he tries to bully you into not even knowing about. He keeps you desperate and insecure so you will accept terrible treatment and consider yourself lucky."

"What do I do?"

"For starters, take what he has offered and replace the numbers with what you are worth," Sarah instructed.

For the next few minutes, Sarah and Johnny revised numbers and discussed clauses, her red pen slashing the document until it fairly bled with conviction. As they worked, Sarah saw Johnny's young shoulders straighten, the light return to his eyes, and the dazzling smile that would shoot him to stardom return to his lips.

"One more tip," she leaned forward. "You are not the one who was supposed to deal with this contract. You have an agent who will be furious that Big Shot tried to dupe you into signing without consultation. Take this contract to your agent, the one who recognizes how valuable you are, and this will never happen to you again."

As Johnny turned to go he paused. "Why are you doing this?"

"Because I once believed those lies and signed my rights away," Sarah stated. "I only wish someone had been brave enough to tell me the truth back then. I didn't believe in myself but you can learn from my mistakes."

"What if Big Shot finds out what you did for me?"

"Oh," Sarah flashed a grim smile, "he will. And I'll lose my job."

Johnny started to protest but Sarah held up a hand to silence him. "It's okay. It's time for me to be free too. Just remember to pay it forward, okay, kid?"

Have you signed a one-sided sexual contract? What lies have you believed about yourself? How have you sold yourself short?

Again, no matter what you've done or what has been done *to* you, you are priceless and worthy of great love.

Like Johnny Talent, I came so close to selling out, to giving up on the dream I'd wanted since, forever, and had planned for since I was fourteen years old. It was just so hard to believe better was "out there" for me. So hard to believe I was worth waiting for.

You may not be a young, budding actor, but regardless, YOU are worth a lifetime of love and commitment. YOU are the one who decides your worth and, therefore, the terms of your "contract."

EXPERT: SPECIALIST, AUTHORITY, PROFESSIONAL, CONNOISSEUR

Nowadays it seems on the edge of extinction for two people to save their most intimate physical experience for marriage. It's so old-fashioned and dull, right?

Wrong.

I'm happily married to my best friend who happens to be the only sexual partner I've ever had and I'm the only one he's ever had. I've NEVER regretted that decision.

Not. Once.

Maybe it seems dull from the outside, but it's not. All those moments of keeping clothing on and choosing to keep hands away from private zones continues to pay off with a thrill of joy that *now we can!* Sex has truly gotten better through the years and, trust me, it started off pretty darn great. Sex, for us, is still a privilege that bonds us together in a way we've never shared with anyone else. It's like two fresh strips of duct tape. Put those together and it's next to impossible to pull 'em apart.

That's the way marriage is supposed to be.

And here's the secret—*It's NOT impossible.*

CHAPTER 3

THE DISEASE

I see them all the time.

Young, blossoming, giggling, flirting, displaying, desperate young ladies convinced the thing that will complete them is sexual adoration. If they just had better hair, tighter abs, poutier lips, and that sexy something whispered about in the pages of fashion magazines, they would get noticed and feel complete.

And the guys? Often, they're looking for a thrill, to make their mark, to feel like a real man, to shake free of authority so they can be in charge. They talk loud, strut, brag and try desperately to avoid the unforgivable sin of the teen male: letting anyone else know how clueless they feel.

And what gems of advice does popular media give these insecure specimens of humanity?

1. To be worthwhile, you must be desired.

2. We all know you're going to do it. When you do, use a condom.
3. It's better if you really love the person—meaning, they turn you on.
4. Unsavory side effects—pregnancy, STDs—can be dealt with medically.
5. If they don't turn you on anymore, dump them. After all, nothing's permanent.

How are they to navigate this hellish minefield of modern dating and emerge on the other side with a healthy self-image and the relational skills to have a thriving, sexy, fun, committed marriage?

Or is the dream of a fulfilling, awesome marriage just another myth set to go the way of Santa and the Tooth Fairy?

Fast-forward five years and what is the typical scenario? Many of those girls have become bitter young women with a string of broken relationships and possibly a divorce and/or abortion under their belt. Older but not wiser, they continue the downward spiral with a number of unsavory options including hatred of the opposite sex, dissolving marriages, brutal legal battles, children caught in the meat grinder of bickering, and another generation learning the ropes of their misery.

For the guys, women have become a necessary evil, a status symbol to convince their peers they've got what it takes to beat their chest and win at any game. Problem is, with a series of sexual escapades behind them, they don't know *how* to be monogamous. Sex, for them, is a selfish affair. This translates into relationships that wither and die because they suck the life out of those who try to gain access to their heart—the true intimacy that would make them *feel* fulfilled when the sex is over.

With all our self-help gurus and therapists making money hand-over-fist, why are we so screwed up?

THE DISEASE

Is there another option besides brokenness and bitterness for young people ready to make decisions that set the course for the rest of their lives?

Yes, and this choice means freedom and stable relationships and the kind of love that makes life bloom with possibilities. It's about helping you get through the confusing maze called "dating" to a happy marriage and amazing sex life that truly lasts for life. But it comes with a large price tag.

It ain't trendy.
It ain't easy.
You won't find it in the glossy pages of *Cosmo* or *GQ*.

WHAT WILL MAKE LOVE LAST?

Someday when you come across the ONE; you know, the person who you truly believe is your soul mate, the love of your life, and you have a chance at true love, what would you want in that relationship? What traits do you think would make it last? Here are some suggestions. (Feel free to add some of your own.)

- Loyalty
- Trust
- Sense of Humor
- Sense of Adventure
- Monogamy
- Forgiveness
- Kindness
- Vulnerability
- Sexual Fulfillment
- Common Spirituality
- Unselfishness
- Grateful Outlook

Those qualities are vital. But what if you had already been burned in every single one of those areas?

It's common for families to be a train wreck these days; mom and dad divorced, blended family, crazy-busy lifestyle, etc. We're already on shaky ground. Add early sexual experience without an understanding of the lifelong ramifications of those choices, and that shaky ground becomes quicksand.

Is it easy to trust when the one you were sleeping with hopped into bed with someone else? Is it easy to be vulnerable and meld your lives together when every other sexual partner crushed your trust and vulnerability into the ground? Is it easy to experience sexual fulfillment when your foundation of sex is steeped in shame, fear and/or even culminated in an abortion?

It's time we realize *sexual freedom* has a hidden price tag: sexual and relational bankruptcy.

It's time for a *Sexual Revolution*—not the "make it free and easy" kind but a "treat it like the treasure it is" revolution.

Please stop believing the lie you are just a pile of out-of-control, raging hormones. You *can* step out of the rapids pulling you toward dead-end relationships and a lifetime of heartache. No, it won't be easy, but ask a couple going through a bitter divorce or a young woman haunted by her decision to end the life of the baby growing inside her. The alternatives are *much* harder.

CHAPTER 4

THE SEXUAL EPIDEMIC

Think of yourself as a clean, sticky strip of duct tape. You're all fresh and fifteen (or younger) and searching for your place in this world while voices from all sides are urging you to hurry up with the bonding.

> "Why do you think you're so sticky?
> You're meant to stick to something. Get after it!"

So you heed the inner and outer voices and find yourself bonded to another young, sticky stripling. Problem is, you're not prepared to remain stuck for life and neither are they. So, in the struggle to get unstuck, chunks of you are left behind. A few more episodes of bonding then ripping away and, even if you try, you're not very sticky anymore. You've become a post-it note of relationships. Your ability to trust dies along with your innocence. Even if you do happen upon the one who could bond with you for life, your experience has prepared you for "temporary" not "permanent."

Easy come. Easy go.

As time goes by, you expect relationships to end and, since you have no practice working through problems in a mature way—since your coping mechanisms remain stuck in the adolescent atmosphere of that first selfish sexual experience—you tend to sabotage relationships as an adult, hauling the baggage of those unhealed, oozing relational wounds.

Without intervention (meaning the aid of an excellent therapist and/or a transforming encounter with God's internal healing) your relationships will continue to end, adding more weight to propel you faster down the hill of despair and loneliness as you bond and un-bond at an ever-increasing rate, trying to discover true intimacy with all your heart, but lacking any ability to *stick*.[1]

Funny how this dead end wasn't disclosed in all those sexy magazines, movies and lyrics that convinced you to be physically intimate as soon as possible. They aren't telling you that we're like that duct tape. We were made to stick. We were created to bond—for life—with *one* other person.[2]

Sex is the superglue. There's actual DNA joining there. Bits of that person, when you have sex with them, remain for the rest of your life. It's the spiritual thing they talk about in marriage services of "the two become one flesh."[3] That deals with much more than just a possible child that could result from sex. We, you and I, all humans, are triune beings—a body with a mind and a spirit. When you join your body, mind and spirit with someone else, that afterimage is left behind not just in your DNA but also in your mind. And the core of you, the Fort Knox of your being—your spirit—is infiltrated as well.

Ever seen the 2004 film *National Treasure*? In the film, there is an incredible series of riddles and elusive clues to protect a treasure of unimaginable proportions. The treasure is so large in fact that most people think it's a myth. But Nicholas Cage's character believes. He believes so much, against incredible opposition, that this belief often puts him at odds with seemingly every sane person on the planet. But he is willing to risk it all for his childlike faith in the unbelievable. In the

---

1 Post from the Onslow Pregnancy Resource Center blog comparing hormones released during sex to the stickiness of duct tape: *Sex And Duct Tape*
2 An in-depth study of the added health, contentment, and fulfilment one experiences with a happy marriage: *The Case For Marriage* by Linda Waite and Maggie Gallagher
3 Mark 10:8; Matt. 19:5; 1 Cor. 6:16; Eph. 5:31

end, of course, he is rewarded with the fulfillment of his dream. He not only finds this immeasurable treasure but is also able to protect it from evil guys who want to steal it.

Imagine you are the one protecting that enormous treasure. This responsibility has been handed down through your family, your great-greats, your grands, your parents, and now it's your turn. You know the history. It's been a huge battle and evil people are constantly trying to get hold of it. Would you trust just anyone? Maybe there'd be a background check any time someone new comes around. You'd want to make it hard for the bad guys to gain access so perhaps there would be a series of tests to weed out those with evil motives.

The fact is, you have a treasure inside far beyond silver and gold. You have a solemn responsibility in your hands. The treasure trove of your body, mind, and spirit are at stake. How careful are you going to be to protect it? It's far more than just you at risk. No less than every child that will come along in your family tree is at the mercy of your choices. Your life, your future happiness, your mate and their future happiness— even the happiness of future generations—are tied up in your choice to either treasure your sexuality or sabotage it with foolish choices.

"But nobody needs to know."
"It's just body parts aligning."
"Wait for marriage? That's SOOO 1950s!"
"Sex will make our relationship better."
"What we do in private is nobody else's business."
LIES!

Want rock solid evidence that "Free and Easy Sex" ain't workin'?

1. 60% of marriages end in divorce.

2. teenpregnancy.org notes that in the U.S. there are 750,000 teen pregnancies each year and 81% of those involve unwed mothers. *(Teenage mothers are more likely to drop out of high school AND they are more likely to be and remain single parents.)*

3. There have been more than 50 million abortions since abortion was legalized in 1973.[4]

4. Antidepressants are the most prescribed drug in the U.S.

5. Suicide is the third leading cause of death for 15 to 24 yr. olds, and is the second leading cause of death for the college-aged group.

6. The rate of suicide for young people 18 to 22 years old has nearly tripled since 1960.

7. Between 500,000 and 1 million young people attempt suicide every year.

---

4   For an excellent compilation of statistics and facts related to teen pregnancy and U.S. abortions, see: 11 Facts About Teen Pregnancy from <u>DoSomething.org</u>

CHAPTER 5

SWEET POISON

"Sickness for the skin—I've got a gift for you
A cancer for within—I've got a gift for you
An ending to begin—I've got a gift for you
and though they're not as nice as the ones you gave to me,
I hope that they will do"
CELLDWELLER - *I'VE GOT A GIFT FOR YOU*

Professor Lyons peered over his spectacles at the eager, young faces before him.

"This island is bursting with life, with species that can be found in only one place—here. As scientists, you have a glorious smorgasbord to discover.

"However, there are seven plants of which you must be warned. I will share them with you in order; least harmful to most deadly."

One-by-one Professor Lyons flashed slides onto the screen. He showed a leaf that would cause a rash, a berry that caused vomiting, a plant that would snap closed, injecting painful nettles. The students took notes, following the professor's words with rapt attention.

Finally, the aged professor leaned against the front of his desk and fixed each aspiring science enthusiast with a piercing gaze. "The last plant is both the most alluring and the most deadly."

Each student looked up, struck by the gravity of his tone.

"Its blossoms explode in every color of the rainbow. The fragrance is intoxicating, both pungent and sweet. Its leaves glimmer in sunlight and glow in darkness and sway even when there is no breeze."

The students, eyes fixed on the professor, hardly breathed as they hung on his words.

Professor Lyons rubbed a tired hand across his brow. "Look at you. I haven't even shown a picture of it and you're captivated; those curious minds eager to unlock its secrets, fingers itching to dissect and discover." He shrugged and shook his head. "I sometimes wonder why I even bother to warn you since this plant is irresistible in every way. It is available throughout the island and is at its blooming peak right now. The Latin name," the professor rolled out a near-unpronounceable word of about fifteen syllables, "is shortened by those familiar with it to 'Siren,' a nod, of course, to the fabled ocean singers who lure unwitting sailors to destruction."

One student shot a hand into the air. "Professor, if it's so deadly, why not just destroy it?"

"Ah! A likely conclusion," he replied, "but your conclusion is based on limited information. Please understand, the Siren is only deadly for a season. Eat its fruit before fully ripened and the negative effects can last for a lifetime and cause a myriad of side effects ranging from paranoia to shortened life span. However," Professor Lyons held up a cautionary finger, "when fully ripened, its fruit and leaves have benefits and healing properties we are just beginning to discover; it calms a troubled mind and brings restful sleep, even slows the aging process. Early studies suggest the Siren is a possible cure for cancer and heals the common cold."

Every hand in the room shot up. Professor Lyons nodded toward a young woman on the back row. "Why isn't this amazing plant being researched worldwide? How can you keep something so potentially beneficial to yourself?"

"Herein lies the true danger," Professor Lyons sighed. "Once someone tastes the Siren's unripened fruit, they not only have the harmful, lifelong ramifications, they also are resistant to the fruit's benefits when at its peak. The fruit even repulses them because they develop a need, a taste for, the unripe fruit, even when its harmful effects are most pronounced."

The room was once more silent as the students pondered his words.

"Seductive and deadly," the professor held open his left hand, "or life-giving benefits to last a lifetime," he opened his right hand. "The simple difference between the two is self-control and patience. Alas, so few hold those virtues in high regard these days, we have almost given up hope of ever discovering all the Siren's secrets."

This is, of course, a thinly veiled analogy for sexual choices. However, the truth applies.

Today's lighthearted attitude toward sex is *very* attractive with promises of fun, excitement, sexy encounters, and the age-old thrill of forbidden fruit. However, we have to remember, poison is created to be irresistible—in order to wipe out its target..

The first apartment Mark and I shared as newlyweds had an ant problem. Basically, the building must have been built atop an entire ant metropolis. I went on the warpath and learned a little trick. Mix enough powdered sugar into the poison, and the ants will cooperate beautifully in their own destruction. Mr. Ant comes along. Yum! He brings his friends. He even takes some home to Queenie. But guess where that free meal ends?

Mass Anticide.

You, my friend, are being poisoned. It's not that sex is poison—what it's mixed with makes it so. The sexy clothing ads, the hot and heavy movies, the steamy TV shows and provocative music lyrics delivered by the coolest, most physically perfect specimens of humanity on the planet combine to convince you: Wow! Sweet! Feels GOOD!

We're just like those clueless ants.

And by the time we see the truth, our life is often so screwed up, we want to die.

KAREN & JIM KROPF

When the boy who'd been saying "I love you" for 3 years, found out Karen was pregnant, he said, "That's too bad for you. You'd better take care of that," and walked away. Panicked and embarrassed, Karen had an abortion. The impact of that decision ultimately led to Karen's eating disorder, chemical dependency and decades of nightmares about the aborted baby.

Thinking an unexpected pregnancy was the worst thing that could happen, Karen went on "the pill". She was horrified when her doctor told her she had chlamydia, a sexually transmitted infection. This Sexually Transmitted Infection is the leading cause of infertility and typically has no symptoms. It wasn't the last time she was infected with it. For Karen, the baby she aborted was the only baby since, as a result of that STI, she was no longer able to become pregnant.

Jim started having sex as a senior in high school, but he never failed to use a condom. As an adult he was devastated to test positive for herpes. His nightmare was to have to tell Karen, the Love of His Life, "I have herpes. If you stay with me, you'll get it too. There's nothing I can do to protect you from it. Please don't leave me."

Now Karen and Jim are motivated by their own heartbreak to challenge young people to rethink their perspectives on sex, love and relationships.

Karen likes to say, "God grows flowers on the manure of our lives." Their non-profit *POSITIVELY WAITING! Inc.,* challenges communities to experience the benefits of sexual self-control.[5]

SELFISHNESS TASTES GREAT—FOR A WHILE

Just because something tastes good, looks good, and feels good, doesn't mean it's good. Ask any drug addict. There's a reason for addiction. The guy who makes money by selling the stuff planned it that way. The drug makes you FEEL GOOD—until you become its slave and it sucks your life away.

Sex outside God's parameters is even more seductive and sneaky than drugs. You'll be convinced no one will ever know, that no STDs and/or no pregnancy means you dodged that bullet. Woohoo! But each step away from God's plan adds another link to the chain of bondage. Pornography and other twisted sexual desires; extramarital affairs that are an atom bomb to your most valued relationships; a shattered, guilt-ridden heart resistant to true intimacy and trust; children raised worshipping the god of immediate gratification who feel so empty—all are waiting for you down that poison road of *not* doing things God's way.

---

[5] To learn more about Karen & Jim Kropf, visit <u>positivelywaiting.com</u>

CHAPTER 6

THE SEXUAL AVALANCHE

Amnon watched Tamar, noting the curves of her body through her flowing gown. His blood boiled when he considered how close she was—the object of his sexual fantasies. For years he had watched her bloom from child to voluptuous woman. Other women were eager for his attentions, but he only had eyes for Tamar. The fact she was his half-sister, well, surely that minor factor could be overlooked. After all, Amnon's father was the king. The king made the laws. As a prince, surely laws made to govern peasants would not apply to him.

Amnon smiled as he considered his own genius plan. He had told the lie he was feeling ill, knowing the soft-hearted Tamar would rush to his side to ease his suffering by preparing his favorite meal. The door to his room was closed. The servants were gone. Tamar brought a platter of steaming food to him, bending down to bring a bite to his mouth. Amnon's hand shot out and grabbed Tamar's

> *wrist, causing the platter to crash to the floor. Though Tamar struggled and screamed in fright, nothing could stop Amnon's lust.*

The Bible records the tale of one of King David's sons, Amnon, who had the hots for his half-sister, Tamar. (2 Samuel 13) He wanted her so much he was miserable and obsessed. He orchestrated an opportunity to get her alone and forced himself on her. Guess what? When he was done using her to satisfy his lust, he couldn't stand the sight of her.

Why?

While there are many possible contributors to his newfound despising of Tamar, my best guess is he hated himself for what he had done and when he looked at her, he saw the reflection in her eyes of the animal he had become.

What to do? "Get her out of my sight!"

Little did Amnon know how much would be ruined by his lust. The ramifications of his selfish actions started an avalanche of ruined relationships and enmity that would continue for generations.

When you choose to go over the edge with someone outside of a legal, lifetime commitment, there are several things you can't control any more than you could a leap off Niagara Falls.

1. **Their immediate reaction**

Does your partner feel guilt? Fear? Self-hatred? Hatred toward you? A clinging neediness since they made themselves so vulnerable? A desire to escape since that vulnerability is frightening?

2. **The fall-out from others**

Do these things *ever* stay between just the two of you? No. One or both of you will talk because, face it, this was a big deal. You'll explode if you can't vent a bit. Beyond that, people will see the signs. Parents aren't stupid. Remember, they were young once too. Close friends will know you're keeping something from them if you try. It's like dropping a pebble into water. Once it leaves your fingers, you have no control over those ripples. The talk, the fear, the possibility of pregnancy or STDs—these are just some of the ripples that will continue for the rest of your life and even into your children's lives and beyond.

3. **The residual emotions**

If I step on a rusty nail, the wound might not appear serious on the outside. It's just one red dot and not much blood to speak of. But, that nail injected poison directly into my bloodstream. Try as I might to cover the puncture with some antibiotic ointment and a band-aid, it's too deep for that. If left untreated and without the intervention of a Tetanus shot, that wound could fester away unseen as millions of microscopic bacteria multiply and wage war on my body. Lockjaw would be a horrific way to die, but that's where I'm headed if I try to ignore that wound.

Sex outside of marriage is much like stepping on that nail. It's a deep connection. And it's a selfish act. Go ahead and hate me for saying it but it's true. No matter how much you try to deny the fact, if you're not ready to commit to that person, to promise them "I'm here for you through sickness and health, wealth or poverty, against all odds," then you are leaving that person vulnerable to emotional fall-out that could undermine every other relationship for the rest of their lives.

"But, it's fate. You can't choose who you fall in love with."

More B.S.

So the first person to make your genitals sit up and take serious notice is your destiny? Seriously? Do you truly have no more self-control than a dog in heat? Is your brain unplugged when your sex drive hits turbo?

Sure chemistry is important and physical attraction is a key component for a satisfying, lasting relationship, *but it's only one factor.*

> "You see how picky I am about my shoes
> and they only go on my feet."
> CHER HOROWITZ FROM THE MOVIE *CLUELESS* DISCUSSES HER VIRGINITY

If the important decision of when and with whom you have sex is based solely on physical attraction, you may find yourself bound to a person who is selfish, weak-willed, an addict, a criminal, or even abusive.

There is hope for a better you, a better relationship, a better future, and a life that spreads hope to others.

In the following pages, we'll discuss tried and true methods of how to <u>NOT</u>:

- Wind up a statistic of teen pregnancy
- Get used and tossed aside
- Lose your self-worth
- Build a backlog of regret
- Equate sex with shame
- Rip your own heart out and hemorrhage the rest of your life
- Destroy your ability to trust
- Destroy your ability to love and be loved
- Leave a trail of destroyed lives in your wake
- Set your future family up for the same hell

The list could go on. It's a life nobody wants. It is avoidable. But you must be forewarned and forearmed.

CHAPTER 7

ONE CHOICE/INFINITE CONSEQUENCES

The mistakes can start pretty young these days. For some, they're already steeped in drugs, sex, and alcohol at the ripe old age of twelve. Ahhh, twelve. I wasn't like that at twelve because, while some are a sex magnet, I was a sex repellant.

The wonderful ugly duckling years. With skinny legs, new braces on my teeth and a bad haircut that turned my waist-length hair into a frizzy, thatched roof, the boy's eyes were NOT on me.

I had another deterrent to sex: *impossibly* old-fashioned parents. They raised us in the country, kept tabs on where we were and whom we were with at all times. So aggravating! Besides, in the small town where I grew up, I'd known those boys since first grade so they were like brothers to me. (Regardless of our reference to Amnon in Chapter 6, ya don't date a brother.)

But even with all these built-in sex deterrents, the time came when I had more freedom, a cute boyfriend, and all the opportunity in the world to get sexually active without a walk down the aisle.

But, lucky for me, something happened between the ugly duckling years and the college boyfriend, something much more important than make-up and a body that remembered it was female. Something that affected the decisions made in the middle of make-out sessions with this guy who *said* he loved me. Why in the world would I refuse to have sex? He was gorgeous, he was fun, he even talked about us getting married. I mean, what's the big deal?

And if I had believed the drivel of our current culture, I too would have inherited the sexual train wreck that's considered "normal."

Not many people talk about the hidden treasures of saving yourself for marriage. But without forewarning and forearming, I never would have made it to my wedding night with the best gift I could give my husband—the same gift he gave me—a body, mind, and spirit that were fresh, open and trusting. It's a gift that, for both of us, has kept on giving (and getting better) over the years.

Don't you owe it to yourself to shoot for the best—the longest life, the healthiest body, the happiest home, love relationships full of trust, a mate so secure in your love they will propel you toward your dreams?

It is possible. But it takes a plan to navigate the romantic minefield.

You might say, "What you do in the bedroom is your own business."

The B.S. monitor goes ballistic.

If that bedroom included every person in your two respective lives affected by your decision to foolishly hop in bed with someone outside a committed, lifelong, legal relationship, the urge to have sex (not to mention the necessary real estate) would be squelched. Total buzz-kill.

Here are just a few who reap the results of your amore.

1. God—He knows better than anybody how far-reaching the fall-out will be.

2. Your parents—whether they have morals or not, what you do reflects on them and, especially if you're young, they might be called upon to raise *your* child.

3. Your friends—your actions make it harder for those around you to stand up for what is right.

4. Children in your life who look to you as a role model—and don't kid yourself—they'll find out sooner or later.

5. Your offspring—what if you make a baby? No telling how many generations will be impacted by your choice to add this person's DNA to your family tree. You're messing with *their* gene pool and they're not even born yet!

6. The possible child who has no choice about the inconvenient timing of their conception and will live with that knowledge (or die due to it).

A TENT THE SIZE OF THE CONTINENTAL UNITED STATES

In the Bible, Abraham was called "friend of God" and "the father of many nations." He was honored with such glowing titles and yet he made a choice that wreaked havoc for future generations.

Abraham is getting to be an old man. God has told him his offspring will "outnumber the stars in the sky." *(Gen. 22:17)* Yet, still, no son—no baby whatsoever.

His wife, since she's in her eighties and has been barren her entire life, devises a plan. She has a servant named Hagar whom she offers to Abraham as a sort of surrogate mother to bear his child. Practically speaking, Abraham can't come up with a better solution, so he takes Hagar as a wife and she becomes pregnant. In due time she gives birth to a son they name Ishmael.

Then Sarah, at the impossible age of ninety, becomes pregnant according to God's prophecy and gives birth to Isaac. From the start, the two sons of Abraham are pitted against each other as bitter rivals since each has a valid right to claim inheritance—Ishmael as Abraham's firstborn and Isaac as the miracle child through whom God will bring the promised Messiah.

It's a no-win situation and the tension between Sarah, Hagar, and their sons becomes unbearable, forcing Abraham to make the horrible decision to send Hagar and Ishmael away with some food and a skin of water. God intervenes, the two live, and Ishmael eventually thrives, establishing the Arab nation since the blessing of Abraham to be the "father of nations" falls on Ishmael as well.

To this day, Abraham's decision resonates in the ongoing rivalry between the Hebrew and Arab nations. Just imagine the size of that tent if Abraham had faced all those affected by his "private" bedroom decision.

Our intimate decisions affect future generations. Two young people groping each other on a secluded road aren't thinking beyond that moment's fulfillment. But God can see beyond physical gratification to the child who, if not aborted, might grow up without a father and perpetuate the problem with instability for future generations. There is always room for God's grace, but it is much harder for a child to trust in God's love when they may believe deep down they are the result of their parents' "mistake."

God can also see beyond that moment to the future of that girl whose life is forever haunted by the repercussions of a thoughtless half hour (or less) of pleasure. Again, there is always room for God's redemption, but she will continue to live the consequences the sexy TV shows never mention: the emotional, financial, social, relational, spiritual repercussions of strolling glibly outside God's plan.

And what about the young man? Best-case scenario, he chooses to be a stand-up guy and not leave the girl to drown. Does he put up the funds for an abortion? Does he marry her even though neither is ready for a long-term, non-selfish relationship? Even if they strive to make mature decisions under difficult circumstances, the demons in their relational closet of guilt, regret, shame, insecurity, etc., are waiting to muddy the already complicated waters of marriage.

> A Belated Thank You
>
> I didn't end up marrying my first serious boyfriend, but I will credit him with one of the most loving statements a girl could ever hear.
>
> When we had been dating for a few months and he was fully convinced my desire to save sex for marriage was serious, he told me, "Chana, even if you begged me to I wouldn't, because someday you would hate me for that."
>
> Ya got that right.
>
> Thank you.

When someone can't keep their hands off you, don't take it as a compliment. Don't take it as a sign of true love that they give in to physical desires. True love will have *your best* in mind, not just for now but for your future.

Decades later, I can look back on my college boyfriend with gratitude because, even though we felt overwhelming passion on many occasions, we don't have the regret of sex to cloud our memories.

If you truly love someone, you won't want the deepest, most vulnerable act they could perform with another person to be shadowed by guilt. An act of selfishness is not a good foundation for any relationship. Even if that person ends up being your life mate, you're leaving a hurdle for yourselves by polluting this most precious of intimate acts with a stain of regret and perhaps the recurring thought, "*Did they not think I was worth waiting for?*" Maybe that wasn't your thought when the hormones were pumping but, once again, you can't control their reaction and, honestly, you *weren't* considering their highest and best when you used their body for your pleasure, or even gave in to *their* pleasure.

> If you truly love someone, you won't want the deepest, most vulnerable act they could perform with another person to be shadowed by guilt.

The dogma that sex is "just an enjoyable pastime" is another big, fat, devastating lie. God tries over and over in the Bible to help us wise up but we're being hit with the opposite message 24/7/365. Which will you believe: the pop stars and actors out to sell you something, or the God who created the gift of sex and has watched mankind screw up time and again for thousands of years?

Victoria Jackson, actress, comic and former Saturday Night Live cast member, learned a vital lesson when she was a struggling, young comic who had just found out her high school sweetheart was marrying another.

"I was mad at God and thought, 'True love doesn't exist so why am I trying to remain a virgin when my true love is marrying someone else?'"

Out of frustration, she told her close friend, "Just do it to me!"

Her friend replied, "I can't because I love you too much. You'd hate me for it later."

Victoria says the true test of someone's love is proven by whether or not they will pressure you to have sex outside a lifetime commitment.

"It's like, if they really love you, they're not going to ask you."

CHAPTER 8

WHAT'S PUSHING YOU TO "JUST DO IT?"

Recently I was doing a search online for "teen questions about sex" and, while I didn't go to anything particularly disgusting, even the relatively logical advice made me wanna puke. While they would say something like, "the only way to ensure no pregnancy is either by abstaining or side-by-side masturbation," the overriding impression was, "This is perfectly natural. You should feel no shame about it. **When** you decide you're ready…" blah, blah, blah.

All of this supposedly well-informed advice steamrolls over the shame aspect, saying it's "normal" to feel shame the first time. Even the "sense of mourning" regarding loss of virginity is just relegated to inexperience and explained away as "perfectly normal." Yeah, right. Just shove down that icky feeling and pretty soon you won't be feeling it anymore. Getting jaded will do that.

The ATEAM is an excellent group I had the honor of working with who spoke to young people about AIDS Awareness and the basics of sexually-transmitted disease prevention. At one point in the presentation, we would display a montage of famous music artists, pointing out how the message in lyrics has morphed from the innocent Beatles line of "I wanna hold your hand," to the graphic, vulgar lyrics of today.

We would ask the students, "Why are these people talking about sex so much?" to which a student would state the obvious, "Because sex sells."

This opened the discussion of the motives of two separate influence groups—those promoting a "casual" attitude toward sex, and those encouraging you to wait. Each faction holds diametrically-opposed motivations for their advice.

The first—media, television, movies, the internet, music, etc.—want to sell you something. Money is the bottom line and sex sells.

The other camp, encouraging you to wait—your parents, the church, true friends, concerned teachers, coaches, etc.—are motivated by what's best for you; your future, your health, your relationships, etc.

Think through the motivation of those pushing you to become sexually active. Some make quite a lucrative living sucking away your innocence. Planned Parenthood is a very influential, vocal proponent of early sexual experimentation and will even receive big bucks if/when one seeks an abortion or "morning after" pill.

Can you say Conflict of Interest?[6]

---

6   Conflict of Interest: a conflict between the private interests and the official responsibilities of a person in a position of trust (Merriam Webster's Dictionary)

You are the one to pay the price of lost health, lost self-worth, lost hope, even the money you spend for their services. In essence, much like the story of Johnny Talent in Chapter 2, you are signing *their* contract that sells *you* short—*way* short.

The old adage "Consider the source" comes into play. Who will suffer with you when your sexual involvement results in an STD, pregnancy, or emotional carnage? The rock stars and Planned Parenthood? No. They only benefit. The ones who would hurt *with* your pain are the ones you need to listen to—ya know, the ones who *care*.

> Don't try to think about what somebody else is doing, what's working for somebody else. Don't try to please your friends or keep up with the Joneses, especially sexually. Don't try to do anything other than what God is directing you to do because not only does God want you to have a "Good" life, He wants to have a "Great" life. And He wants you to have a great sex life.
>
> WONDER-HUBBY MARK

Victoria Jackson was nineteen when she made her first trip to Hollywood with sky-high ambitions in tow. Her friend we mentioned before, let her crash at his place while she looked for work. The first night, her friend was surprised when Victoria insisted on sleeping on the couch. "He thought I was kidding, but I wasn't. I told him, 'I'm a Baptist virgin and I'm stayin' that way.'"

Victoria stuck with that lifestyle for two years, but she realizes now that her focus was on making it as an actress and paying the bills rather than finding a good church and growing spiritually. "All the things I had been taught are wrong like drinking, smoking and (casual) sex were all around me and looking less and less shocking all the time."

Then came the news from home that her high school sweetheart Paul, whom she thought she was going to marry, was marrying someone else. "I just thought, 'True love doesn't exist, so what's the point?'" She gave in to a friend with a bohemian lifestyle who had been pressuring her to have sex.

The first thing he told her afterwards was the name of the gynecologist he "took all his women to."

"I was twenty-one and I gave my virginity to a fire-eater gypsy hippie and he threw it in the garbage can!" Victoria says with an exasperated roll of her famous blue eyes. She says the first thing the gynecologist said when they walked into his office was, "How's so-and-so?" referring to the last woman her new lover had brought there. "My heart just cracked," said Victoria.

Soon Victoria realized, even as her career was taking off, that she was dying inside. "I was taking him to church and he was giving me pot. I was taking him to church and I was having a nervous breakdown and starting to drink vodka in the morning."

Once, her boyfriend called Victoria's father and said, "Vicky's crying all the time!" to which her father retorted, "That's because she's living in sin! If you'd marry her, she'd stop crying!"

So Victoria's fire-eater proposed. "He had never believed in marriage, but then I started getting TV work so he started to believe in marriage."

Victoria explains her decision to accept his proposal this way. "I was thinking, 'A Christian man won't want me because I'm a whore and, if I marry him, I'm not a whore because he's the only man I've been with.' I couldn't get it in my head that God could forgive me."

"Seven years of hell," is Victoria's description of that marriage. "When I got pregnant he said, 'Do you want to keep it or lose it?' All I could say was, 'You don't even know me!'"

As Victoria's career bloomed, her marriage grew increasingly unbearable until her husband's erratic behavior convinced her it was dangerous for her and her young daughter to remain with him.

Victoria's marriage ended as her career was shifting into high gear. "When he said he wanted custody of our daughter, I didn't even try to fight him over money, I just told him, 'Take it all, but leave my daughter out of it!'"

(We'll read more about Victoria's long road back to healing in the chapter titled "I Screwed Up. Now What?"

As Victoria stated with a snicker, "I'm the poster child for that one!")

I knew a young lady in college, we'll call her Natalie, who was still a virgin at twenty-one. Like me, she greatly anticipated marriage and sex, but she had held strong even though she had a natural gift of flirting with guys that was truly an art. Add to that her beautiful eyes and 1000-watt smile and, yeah, bees to honey.

Then came the gorgeous guy she met in a college class. He was tall, handsome, intelligent, and full of charisma. In fact, everything about this young man seemed to scream, "Here is the perfect male!" My friend, amazed at her good fortune in attracting this glorious specimen of manhood, began dating him. After several months, when she was convinced she was "in love" and they had even discussed marriage, Natalie became sexually involved.

Imagine her horror when she met someone who, when they realized she was a friend of Mr. Perfect, inquired after his wife.

For years after dating Mr. Already-Married, this formerly effervescent and confident young lady struggled with paranoia, panic attacks, and low self-image. When she did marry, she chose someone who had a habit of lying. Natalie admitted she feared no one else would ask her.

With one choice of sexual bonding outside of marriage that resulted in betrayal, this optimistic young woman became a haunted, fearful young lady who accepted bad treatment and even chose to marry someone who made her life miserable. When the marriage eventually ended in divorce, she and her children were left with horrendous scars.

That sexual bonding with a lying, married guy—an experience she described as "so beautiful" at the time—was a poison dart to her soul and to her future.

Natalie has grown through the pain and has relied on God, her anchor in the storm. I asked Natalie, if she could have a do-over, would she make the same choice about that first sexual encounter?

Her answer: "Heck no! I'd run so fast his head would spin! Maybe *after* I kicked him where it counts!"

―――――

But sexual temptation doesn't have to be the result of dating a married jerk or immersing yourself in the Sin City of Hollywood. All it takes is a touch of compromise.

Remember my shiny vow to remain a virgin until marriage? Well, I had four years to smugly believe that vow would be a piece of cake to maintain. Then came college. Suddenly I was dating cute guys who didn't know what a geek I had been in junior and senior high. Suddenly I had a boyfriend who was handsome and fun and who even said he was a Christian. I knew he wasn't committed to pleasing God in every area of his life, but what could it really hurt, right? It was just a date. Then two. Then a couple of dates a week. Then we agreed to date exclusively. Suddenly there was desire and opportunity and someone who knew how to kiss in such a way that made me want more. Suddenly sex no longer sounded disgusting. Suddenly I wanted to be touched in those ways I had vowed would not happen until marriage.

After about a year and a half, I had to deal with the fact that, wonderful as this guy was, we would not make a happy marriage. We chose to break off our relationship, though it hurt us both deeply, because it was foolish to remain in a relationship tempting toward sex, when lifetime commitment was not really a consideration.

Would that action have been even more devastating if we had become sexually active? Definitely. In fact, it might have been almost impossible due to pregnancy or the deep bonding that would have made us both feel obligated to marry. And who knows what physical repercussions there might have been, since he had gone through a promiscuous era in his early college years.

I'm not proud of all my actions in that college relationship. I wish to this day I hadn't made things worse by dating him as long as I did. But I thank God that clothing remained on (even when I needed cold showers), and that my boyfriend respected my desire to remain a virgin until marriage.

RECOMMENDED READING:

And the Bride Wore White by Dannah Gresh

Sex Makes People Stupid: How To Avoid Ending Up With A Loser by Karen Kropf.

Karen and Jim Kropf's website is a wonderful source of powerful, up-to-the-minute information and advice: positivelywaiting.com

CHAPTER 9

THE ENEMY WITHIN

Stephanie didn't look like a promiscuous girl. In fact, she was just darn lovable with her effervescent personality, blonde curls and gorgeous smile. But Stephanie carried the weight of being the result of her parents' teenage pregnancy, thus she never felt wanted. The only thing that touched that pain? Physical affection—that she equated with love. So Stephanie became sexually active as a teenager and eventually married an abusive, selfish man. A daughter and son were born to them and Stephanie, not wanting the harmful atmosphere for her children, got out of the marriage that had left her with even more emotional scars and self-image issues.

When she met Jason, a wonderful man who gave rich love and acceptance to her and her children, Stephanie couldn't resist. Again she became sexually involved outside of marriage. Eventually, she discovered she was pregnant.

After discussing their options, she and Jason realized they were not ready for marriage. The choice that seemed to make the most sense? Abortion.

Soon Stephanie and Jason found themselves hesitating outside an abortion clinic. Jason broke the silence.

"We can't do this."

With a sigh of relief, Stephanie agreed.

They took the necessary steps to arrange adoption for their child.

Eventually, Stephanie and Jason married. They have maintained contact with the child they conceived and decided not to abort—a boy raised in a stable, loving home.

Together, Stephanie and Jason are raising three children, the two from her previous marriage, and another conceived after they wed.

Do the old wounds and decisions pose hurdles for them spiritually and relationally? Yes. But they are relying on the truth of scripture and their relationship with God to fill in the gaps.

Do they talk to their kids about sexual decisions?

"All the time," says Stephanie. "We as parents have got to be the ones our kids hear this stuff from. My teenage daughter, my oldest, knows that God has a better way and that I'm gonna stay on her to treasure her sexuality for her husband. She's an awesome kid who knows we adore her."

Jason chimes in. "I'm like the techno cop. I go through their emails and check their phones and scan the songs on their playlists. These days, ya can't let your guard down a second."

Most often, like Stephanie, it's what's going on *inside* our heads—our needs and fears—that propel us toward sexual promiscuity. There's an emotional itch that nothing else seems to scratch. Problem is, like that hit of cocaine or meth that can make folks feel on top of the world, the great feeling is temporary. But the act of uncommitted sex opens a Pandora's box of repercussions that affect the rest of your life.

And here's the diabolical truth: everybody suffers, especially the children who bear the brunt of those choices. Mom had a fling and got pregnant. That baby grows into a child who never quite feels wanted and may never even know the biological father. That's some hefty holes in the foundation of a kid's self-worth.

Even if your parent's sexual mistakes don't prompt you to repeat them, their sexual fallout still affects every aspect of your life.

Tina was six when her dad left her mom for another woman. Her childhood was a blur of a stressed-out mom who yelled a lot, an angry older brother who screamed at her overwhelmed mom—and no dad—no matter how bad things got.

When Tina was eighteen she had a very rare conversation with her father, the gist of which was, "I'm busy with my new family. Please don't ever ask me for anything."

In her romantic life, this affected Tina in several ways. First, when a young man was interested in her, even talking marriage, Tina assumed he wasn't serious. She had a deep conviction she was just a passing fancy and the young man in question would move on. In the one or two relationships when a guy would convince her he was trustworthy and wasn't running away, she found herself with such a deep need for emotional reinforcement, the young man would realize she needed more than he could give and he would opt out. Even though Tina has preserved her sexuality through long years of hoping and praying for the right man, this beautiful woman with a body most women would pay big money to achieve admits she is convinced there must be something freakish about her that would gross a guy out, *if* she ever allowed him close enough to discover it.

As far as spirituality, her relationship with God is marked by the same fear. She knows God is the only one Who can heal the wounds inflicted by her father's absence, but she constantly struggles with the belief that God doesn't have time for her or that she is not worthy of His attention. On an even more fundamental level, she believes there is something about her that begs rejection, *even by the most loving being in the universe.*

The deep wound left behind by Tina's father? Rejection.

Laura is a young woman who grew up heavily involved with church. Problem was, as she entered her teen years, she found she was attracted sexually, not to the guys, but to other girls. At her church, the topic of sex was never discussed. Ever. She had misgivings about her sexual leanings but she felt if she talked to anyone she would be rejected therefore she withdrew. As her frustration and sexual desires became more pronounced, she found emotional release by cutting herself. While the self-injury seemed to be an outlet for her pain, it was one more thing to hide from the world, therefore Laura felt more and more isolated from her friends and family.

When her best friend in college finally became her girlfriend, Laura thought some of the pain would subside, but her cutting just got more and more out of control. Finally, when her girlfriend dumped her, Laura could no longer hide her pain. Luckily, this time she went to a therapist who wasn't fazed by the cutting but told her to utilize things like writing or finding a good friend to talk to when the urges to cut were driving her crazy. As the secrets seeped out like sand through her fingers, Laura was thrilled to discover friends who stuck by her.

"They showed me what healthy relationships look like instead of just trying to explain them to me. They answered my questions about boys and girls and life. They stayed silent and let me rant when I was angry. They were truly Christ on earth for me."

Laura says she still struggles with inner pain, but when the hard times hit, she writes out her feelings and has the support of wonderful friends. Through it all she has discovered deep love and acceptance from God.

"God is not waiting for you to clean up your act and follow Him," says Laura. "He is down in the dirt and grime of life with you, holding you up and just waiting for you to recognize Him."

Sometimes, shame is caused by someone else's actions. We can't always control what happens to us—even circumstances from before our birth or from childhood—and emotional wounds are powerful motivators pushing us to obey our feelings rather than what is right in God's eyes and best for our future.

In my early twenties, I dated a young man who seemed perfect for me. I became more and more convinced I had finally found Mr. Right. Then suddenly, when we had been dating exclusively for three months, he pulled away. I was very hurt but was in no mood to pursue someone who treated me as if I had the plague. A couple months later he called me on the phone and confessed the problem. When he was a child, an older family friend had molested him. Ever since, he had struggled with shame and questioned his sexual leanings.

About a year later, another wonderful guy, another three months of bliss and hope then BAM! He's back-peddling from me as if I had sprouted horns. A few weeks later, we sat in a car as he gripped the steering wheel and looked anywhere but into my eyes as he confessed—as a child he was molested by a man who was a family friend and ever since... you know the rest.

My heart still hurts for these young men, but I'm grateful they both cared enough to be honest with me. I can only hope and pray opening up to me made it easier to seek professional, God-centered help.

Do I share these stories to slam the homosexual community? No. In fact there are folks of that community whom I love deeply. But I must make an appeal. Even an attraction to the same gender doesn't divorce you from morality. Your sexual choices don't just affect you. Every encounter begins an avalanche of repercussions.

Did God give us His laws just to boss us around? No. He created sex. He *gave* you this great gift.

Jeremiah 29:13 says, "For I know the plans I have for you," declares the Lord, "Plans to prosper you and not to harm you, to give you a hope and a future."

God wants what's good for you. Just like heterosexuals having affairs, if you have homosexual affairs, you are giving away chunks of yourself, taking chunks from others, and leaving devastation in your wake.

I don't have all the answers and there is much about this topic that remains a mystery to me. I can say with total confidence that God's love is boundless. He loves us forever, regardless of our sexual choices, with a passion that makes our human passions pale in comparison. Therefore, whether homosexuality is born or caused, is not for me to decide. My place is not to condemn, because Jesus' life, death, and resurrection announced a new day and a new covenant where God took care of *our* part of the covenant as well.

Jesus, declared, **"I have come that they may have abundant life."** [7]And all His actions while on the earth—ALL—were loving toward those He

---

7   John 10:10

met, regardless of what they had done. The only ones to receive the brunt of Jesus' anger? Smug religious leaders who tried to keep people away from God with their heavy weights of law and condemnation. Jesus' actions speak for themselves. His love pursues all of us, even those counted as today's "lepers, prostitutes and tax collectors." Think about it. *He went to find them.*

For some time now, I have been convinced the next great move of spiritual revival will spark into wildfire among the homosexual community. What joy to witness AIDS victims freed from any trace of HIV! God's love is big enough but so many of us, like Tina, are convinced we are rejected and forgotten. My job is to declare that God's love is able to reach into the core of us, filling our deepest need and releasing us from the prison of shame.

Perhaps you are a Christian who is tormented by powerful homosexual urges. I am no expert on this issue, but, again, I KNOW God loves ALL. PERIOD.

The key is to give yourself unreservedly to Christ. Ask Him to search out those deep recesses of poison that push you toward harmful decisions. Ask Him to fill your emotional black hole. Then:

- Read the Bible.
- Study Jesus.
- Fall in love with Him.
- Bathe your mind with His words, memorizing the Bible in little chunks (or big ones).
- Get alone with God every day, setting time aside for His healing and for Him to breathe His love over your life.
- If there are ways you are disobeying His desires, ask for His strength to please Him *above all things*.

If you've never asked Jesus to take over your life, there's no time like the present. Feel free to use the following prayer as a model.

> Dear God,
>
> I give you my life. I ask You to take over. I accept that Jesus' blood, shed on the cross for all people, has bought new life for me. Through Him, I am a new creation, no longer a slave to those things that hurt You because they separate us.
>
> Today is the first day of a new life. I am no longer my own. I am Yours. Help me in the process to renew my mind (Romans 12:1-2) so negative emotions and thoughts no longer control it.
>
> I say that Jesus is the Son of God with my mouth and I choose to believe that fact in my heart (Romans 10:9). Today, Jesus is my Savior and my Lord.
>
> Thank You, Heavenly Father, for making me your child.
>
> In Jesus' holy name I pray.
>
> Amen.

Use your own words if you prefer. And if, or when, you choose to pray to receive Christ, *mean it*. Just know that day is the first day of a completely new life.

The choice to pray may seem simple, but don't be surprised at the backlash ahead. Satan will do whatever he can to put you back in chains, whether it's a call from old friends offering drugs, an old love showing up desiring a tumble, or just old thought patterns pushing you into despair. Continue to *choose* what's right and seek out reinforcement from other sincere believers. There's strength in numbers. When you're at the end of your rope, those friends will pray for you and vice versa.

We all have the deep desire and need to be loved—fully known *and* fully loved. Truth is, even with the most wonderful of life partners, the need goes deeper than they can reach. Besides, that person cannot be everywhere at once therefore they can't *always* be there for you. And, they don't know everything; therefore they can't understand the core of your emotional need. To top it off, that person doesn't have the *power* to reach inside and heal your wounds.

Those abilities are called omnipresence (everywhere at once), omniscience (knows everything), and omnipotence (all-powerful). Those qualities only belong to One—God. If we don't accept His help to address our emotional wounds, we will demand that people—or one special person—be what only God can be. It's a recipe for relational failure.

No matter where you are right now and no matter what your particular battles, God is there and He loves you more than you could ever imagine. Seek Him first every minute of every day and keep a constant check on what is the first priority of your life. God has said that if we will delight in Him, He will give us the desires of our hearts—and if we trust Him enough to hand over our lives to Him—we will *find* true life.

Grab hold of that promise and never let go. His love is what your heart craves.

RECOMMENDED READING:

The Battlefield of the Mind by Joyce Meyer

Stronger by Brian "Head" Welch—daily devotions for growing in the Christian walk:

Exodus International is a ministry reaching out in love to the homosexual community. Laura's story is taken from their website:

CHAPTER 10

DEADLY SEXUAL STUMBLING BLOCKS

"Above all else, guard your heart,
for it affects everything you do."
Prov. 3:27 (NET)

IS YOUR WINDSHIELD DIRTY?
THE IMPORTANCE OF YOUR WORLDVIEW

A belief system is a set of intangible parameters we erect in our minds that help us understand the way things are—at least the way we *think* things are. So how can what we think affect what's real? For instance, if I choose to believe there's no intelligent design to the universe, that I just happened to exist by a strange series of coincidences and that what is unseen doesn't exist, those beliefs are just in my head and can't harm anyone, right?

A purely human-centric, me-centered point-of-view is called selfish. If there's no moral code, no right and wrong, and this short life is all the chance I get to experience everything I can get my greedy hands on, my life will resemble a steamroller. Pity the fool who tries to stand between me and my desires.

Unfortunately, this sounds a lot like the world in which we live. I'm not saying by a long shot that the "good ol' days" were perfect. Wars and strife and crime have always been a part of mankind's history. But our world today has flipped. Right is wrong and the only true wrong is those who have the audacity to believe certain truths are not malleable according to the latest fashion.

But stop and think for a moment what a humanist/purely-science-devoid-of-a-moral-code viewpoint does to the way we view ourselves.

If there is no higher power or God, then it's up to me to call the shots. How do I call those shots? I follow instinct and emotions. But my emotions are fickle and leave me on shaky ground. Plus, since I am just a cosmic accident, other people are rather cheap. We are basically animals with opposing thumbs. Why should we deny ourselves any pleasure since we live such a short time anyway? If the person I'm with no longer aids me in my selfish aims, then I should move on to someone else who will. Get the picture?

In that type of worldview, what is stable and trustworthy?

Nothing.

Who can I count on to stay by my side when I'm down?

No one.

Do the choices I make matter in the grand, cosmic soup of human existence?

Nope. The whole mess is just empty and meaningless.

Yes, this is a simplified explanation of a humanistic worldview, but just look around. This is basically the world we live in. What's *un*usual these days is selflessness and sacrifice to meet the needs of others.

Think about it. Who are the happiest people on Earth? If selfishness is a recipe for happiness then the U.S.A. should have that market cornered. But evidence is to the contrary. The happiest people invest themselves in others and gain an intangible but fulfilling satisfaction by making a difference, by improving someone else's lot. This defies logic but it's true.

Regardless of a possible afterlife, what sounds better?

1. Taking your last breath surrounded by a loving, committed family and friends who have gone through thick and thin with you?

2. Dying alone because no time in life was "wasted" investing in others?

But even with the evidence of countless empty lives wasted by an endless pursuit of personal happiness, the humanist worldview continues to acquire more avid fans. And while the lack of morals in a godless society removes sticky impediments to selfish pursuits, we as a society *are not getting happier.* In fact, divorce rates are at an all-time high, suicide abounds, pornography infects every facet of our lives, human trafficking is off the charts, while heart disease, AIDS, cancer, diabetes and every other debilitating disease thrives in pandemic proportions. What gives?

In an article exploring the high suicide rate of Las Vegas, Nevada (according to the study, people who live in Las Vegas have twice the risk of committing suicide than any other city in the U.S.) a quote at the end of the article sums up the situation well. Las Vegas is marked by, "social isolation, fragmentation and low social cohesion, all of which have long been identified as correlates of suicide."[8]

Notice these three components:

1. Social Isolation
2. Fragmentation
3. Low Social Cohesion

What has been the mainstay of social cohesion throughout human history? The nuclear family.

What does a society riddled by divorce and short-term trysts rather than lifelong commitment cause? Fragmentation.

What does a pursuit of personal happiness at the expense of other's needs accomplish? Social Isolation.

Therefore, while a humanist, purely scientific worldview sounds logical on the surface and can seem harmless in its implications, this widely accepted philosophy has accomplished several devastating results.

1. The cheapening of human life: If we're just a cosmic happenstance, there's no reason to feel awe for the miracle of life—my own or another's.
2. The cheapening of life choices: If this short life is all there is then "let's eat, drink, and be merry for tomorrow we die."
3. The cheapening of key relationships: Who has time to figure out psychological wounds that hinder intimacy? Keep things short-term and uncomplicated.

---

8   Study funded by the Robert Wood Johnson Foundation Health & Society Scholars program and published in the Las Vegas Sun. Read the entire article here: lasvegassun.com/news/2008/nov/13/just-being-vegas-raises-risk-suicide-study-finds

4. A populace with no direction, no foundation and no moral backbone. It's each one for himself—a society of users.

Belief in God and moral absolutes has become less popular at an alarming rate. In fact, the speed with which we've progressed from a God-fearing nation to a God-sneering one could not have been more rapid if it had been orchestrated to perfection (a fact worth pondering).

Here's the deal. The spiritual world is real. We can't see, measure, or otherwise scrutinize that world in a scientific manner any more than we could take the love between a man and woman, mix it in a beaker with other substances, and separate its components. But what is intangible is absolutely vital to a meaningful life since what we *think* provides the lens through which we *perceive* our world. Ask a dried up, depressed, bitter old man on his deathbed with no significant loved ones if life is full of hope, joy and love. More than likely his outlook will be bleak. Why? Because perception creates reality. There comes a time when our perspective is so poisoned, we're blind to the intangibles of hope, joy, and real love.

I'm reminded of a wonderful speech by the lawyer who defends Kris Kringle in the classic movie, *A Miracle on 34th Street*, when the woman he's interested in berates him for believing in what seems impossible. He tells her, "Someday you're going to find that your way of facing this realistic world just doesn't work. And when you do, don't overlook those lovely intangibles. You'll discover they're the only things that are worthwhile."

Recently I heard a pastor on the radio who had been at the bedside of many dying people in his years of ministry. He had witnessed two forms of grief:

1. Grief from those left behind who would miss their loved one.
2. Grief because those still living knew the deceased's life had been wasted.

Why am I including a downer chapter about a humanist mindset in the middle of a book about achieving an exciting life filled with love?

Because our beliefs guide our actions.

You are unique, priceless, and adored by an ever-present, omnipotent, always-loving God who hurts when you hurt, has wonderful plans for your life, and wants you to live a life of fulfilling significance. If you understand your worth from God's point-of-view, you're less likely to sell out to someone whose motives are to use you for a momentary thrill. If you can grasp how desperately you are loved by the God of the whole universe, security, confidence, and overflowing love will be the defining characteristics of your life choices. A person who's fulfilled on the inside lives a life of stability because their deepest needs are met. They're no longer compelled to suck the life out of relationships in a desperate attempt to fill an emotional black hole.

PORNOGRAPHY

Blaine was a leader in his church and had been a powerful influence in the Christian community for years. But he had a secret. Blaine had a powerful addiction to pornography that had raged out of control until he was no longer satisfied with just images on a screen but craved to experience those actions for himself. But one day, the walls of his lies and hidden sexual life crashed down around him.

***His wife and children were devastated. His church reeled from the scandal....*[9]**

It's everywhere, destroying lives worldwide like the Black Plague. Like our earlier analogy of the rusty nail, pornography pierces a deep, abiding, lethal wound on our hearts, minds, spirits, libidos, emotions, relationships, and self-worth.

Perhaps the devastation of pornography is not so evident as an addiction to meth that visibly ravages its victims at an alarming rate, but pornography's poisonous wounds are just as brutal. From wives unable to compete with the airbrushed "other woman," to men hiding their shame, daughters whose wounds compel them to display their bodies, and children trapped in the slavery to adults attempting to satisfy twisted appetites, pornography's legacy creates a living hell and erodes relational and societal stability at the core.

In fact, pornography is so pervasive, just one click on the computer can kick the lid off this cesspool. As a mom and wife prayerfully desiring to guard the minds and hearts of our family, pornography is the constant, persistent burglar clawing at every crack to gain access. I have cried with friends and family members who confessed to stumbling upon pornography in a bookstore or website. They felt dirty. They hid their shame. It was an instant craving they both hated and coddled. We have prayed and cried and prayed some more. Wonderfully, God is always ready to receive a repentant heart and those wounds, though painful, can be turned, through God's love, into strength.

---

[9] Read Blaine's story: <u>Death by a Thousand Lies: My Cover Up, My Crash and My Resurrection from Sexual Addiction</u> by Blaine Bartel

Again, we have an enemy who understands all too well the importance of foundations. He also understands the strength a husband and wife can find in their exclusive, holy act of marital lovemaking. Satan's constant desire is to erode our concept of sex. He desires, as early as possible, to inject shame, kill our self-worth, and infect us on an emotional level so we either: a) cannot find fulfillment with our mate or b) are repulsed by this act that, from our first sexual experience, brought deep pain and shame.

Karen Kropf, speaks about sexual self-control through her organization, Positively Waiting.[10]

In her presentation, Karen shows the picture of a trail of baby ducklings following a dog. It illustrates the concept of "imprinting." When a baby duckling is born, whatever or whoever is the first thing he sets his little duck eyes on, even if it's not the mother, is what he follows.

Karen explains this is what happens with a young man's first sexual experience. If his first sexual encounter was riddled with fear, danger and risk (such as his girlfriend's house with the possibility her father might arrive home and kill him) *this* is what he imprints on sexually. Thus he seeks these components as the road to sexual climax in the future—fear, danger, and risk.

Ever wondered about the man who appears to have it all—beautiful wife, kids, affluence, community respect—who risks it all with repeated affairs? There's the explanation. He has imprinted, not on the women who give him their bodies, but rather on the fear, danger, and risk he seeks for a "fulfilling" sexual experience.

---

10 Visit Karen's website: positivelywaiting.com

But there is healing for thoughts, beliefs, and even sexual scars that impact our ability to maintain a thriving, lifelong love relationship. It's not easy. In fact, Brian "The Head" Welch of Korn fame says in his book *Stronger* that he had the image of Christ tattooed on the palm of his hand to prevent the urge to masturbate.

Now that's commitment to change!

Author Jonathan Welton was a minister, husband and father with a secret porn addiction. When he sought help, he felt labeled as a sex addict who would *always* be an addict fighting powerful sexual appetites. This did not ring true to Jonathan who knew the Bible and God well enough to know this was not God's best for him, that God's healing would bring true transformation to enable him to live free of porn's seductive pull.

If you or someone you know struggles with pornographic addiction (or addiction of any kind for that matter) Welton's book, *Eyes of Honor*, offers a clear path of escape out of a self-destructive cycle.

RECOMMENDED READING:

Eyes of Honor by Jonathan Welton

Visit positivelywaiting.com to learn more about Karen Kropf's life-changing presentations, books and other resources: http://positivelywaiting.com

Stronger by Brian Welch:

Death by a Thousand Lies: My Cover up, My Crash and My Resurrection From Sexual Addiction by Blaine Bartel

CHAPTER 11

BELIEVING THE IMPOSSIBLE

THE TALE OF LESTER AND ESTHER

One day when he was a young man, Lester saw a stunning gal strolling down the street and announced to his buddies, "See that girl over there. I'm gonna marry her."

Soon Esther and Lester were dating and head-over-heels in love. Problem was, Esther's parents didn't approve of Lester. He had been married before when he was very young and divorce wasn't acceptable to them. Finally, Esther and Lester eloped. For six months, Esther continued to live at home as she tried to work up the courage to break the news to her parents. When she finally told them, her father said, "Thought that boy never was gonna get around to it."

For more than fifty years, Lester and Esther remained each other's best friend and biggest fan; through good times and bad, through sickness and health, through riches and poverty.

One night in 1986, Lester went to bed… and never woke up. Three years later, Esther sat in her easy chair and related the story with a smile even as she reached for another Kleenex to dab at her eyes.

"That night, as he got up to go to bed, he came over to my chair. The last words he ever said to me were, 'Do you know how much I love you?' Then he kissed my cheek and said, 'And do you know how beautiful you are?'"

Esther grinned, wrinkled her nose and flashed her aging-movie-star smile. "We were so blessed."

Sounds like next year's hit chick-flick, huh. But Esther and Lester are their real names and this is a real story of two people who remained gloriously in love for a lifetime. In fact, Esther and Lester were my husband's maternal grandparents. Their love provided a haven for Mark when his childhood home was torn by divorce. Their relationship inspired him to desire the same kind of love in his own life. Their practice of habitual kindness to each other showed Mark how to keep love fresh and fun, and what elements *do not* belong in a healthy relationship.

My Grandmommy and Granddaddy (Esther and Lester) were a great picture of unconditional love. They were just so sweet to each other all the time. You could tell they still did it for each other... they had it bad for each other.

They were the 50-years-down-the-road couple that I wanted to be like. I got to see stability with them.

I wanted to model after their borderline-syrupy relationship. I just knew that's what I wanted. I think having other marriages around me fall apart, their relationship was my beacon.

WONDER-HUBBY MARK

Deep, unselfish love that gets richer as the years go by is possible. It's one of the beautiful intangibles that makes life worth living. The problem is, nowadays this kind of love is so rare that most treat it like a fairytale—fun to dream about but not based in reality. Thank God for the Lesters and Esthers of this world who are foolish enough to prove the rest of us wrong.

PASSION

Bono, lead singer of U2, has a great definition of "passion." Passion, he says, is the combination of love and anger.

> Are you angry enough to fight for love?
>
> Are you willing to shake up everything you've been taught about true passion?
>
> Are you childlike enough to believe in fairytales?

In the armed forces, Marines are called "the few, the proud." They gain that title through tons of hard work, discipline, gut-wrenching sacrifice, and a commitment to something that eclipses their immediate gratification.

Now consider the most important things you will look back on when you're on your deathbed. What legacy do you want to leave behind? If you are one of the few, you long to leave this world a bit better than you found it with a legacy of hope, stability, and exciting, loving, fulfilling relationships for the generations to come.

If this is truly your desire, the journey will require discipline, hard work, gut-wrenching sacrifice, and a commitment to goals that eclipse immediate gratification.

If you're angry enough to be radical, you've come to the right place. You're in shark-infested waters, but with a clear goal and a clear plan to get you there you can, with God's help, be equipped for survival.

In the following chapters, we'll discuss a few key elements that could very well make the difference between a lifetime of regret or living your own fairytale.

Have you ever heard these words?

> "Gee. If only I had been sexually active at a younger age."
>
> "I wish I'd had the memory of more guys' moans in my head on my wedding night."
>
> "I feel incomplete because I missed the thrill of pre-marital sex."
>
> "I really wish I could have had sex with him before we broke up and never saw each other again."

I haven't.

But I've heard these phrases many times:

> "If only I had waited."
>
> "If only I could forget."
>
> "If only I could feel clean again."
>
> "I really regret I wasn't a virgin on our wedding night."
>
> "Why did I let that jerk talk me into that? I didn't even like it!"
>
> "I feel like they took a chunk of me I'll never get back."

You owe it to yourself to think about irreversible actions before you buy the lie that it's "no big deal." You could walk out the door and choose to lose your virginity any day.

Now walk out that same door and get it back.

CHAPTER 12
THE WAITING GAME

WAIT

For today's generation, that tops the list of four-letter, dirty words. We live surrounded by symbols of our impatience.

> Hungry? Drive-through for a burger.
> Broke? Get an instant loan.
> Bored? Download a TV show or shoot people in a computer game.
> Lonely? Grab a cell phone to chat or text.
> Out of shape? Get lipo.

Interpretation: we're instantly gratified **but not deeply satisfied**.

We're so accustomed to the Mickey D's drive-through lifestyle we've forgotten what deep satisfaction tastes like.

Problem is, as any investment advisor will tell you, shallow investment equals shallow returns. Even worse, if you choose to fritter your treasure away, soon you'll have nothing to save or share.

My husband and I accompanied a small group of friends from our church to build a home in Mexico. The philosophy of the organization we worked with is to use only the tools available to the locals—no cement mixer, no electric saws or nail guns—everything is done the old-fashioned way of hands-on, hard, manual labor. We lugged buckets of rock and cement mix, stirred and spread concrete, sawed boards, and pounded nails until we were coated in a thick layer of sweat and grime.

But, at the end of those few days of manual labor alongside some of the beautiful, local children, I realized I'd never felt dirtier, more tired, more ready for a hot shower (facilities at the campsite did not include running water) *or* more satisfied by a job well done. Friendships among our crew blossomed with the hard work and laughter-filled meals we shared around the campfire. Although the photo of our group posing in front of the work site showed a motley crew, the contented smiles of satisfaction were genuine.

Sure a cement truck would have been easier but what was saved in time and effort would have been lost in *effectiveness*. The locals needed to see these pampered, middle-class Americans working and sweating alongside them, and we needed the experience of building something with our own hands that stretched and strengthened us.

You see, we've gotten so used to quick mediocrity, we've forgotten the deep fulfillment of persistence and excellence. To have a dream, to set the goal, to focus and sacrifice in order to achieve that goal, makes the victory an unforgettable experience that stays with you for a lifetime because—

The Greater the Investment, the Greater the Reward.

If we had set up a pre-fab, tin building it would have done the job, for a while, but the integrity of a home established with sweat, backbreaking labor and teamwork just, well, *means more and stands stronger*. The pre-fab building would have no emotional tie for me. However, if I visit that site tomorrow, I would be overwhelmed with memories: laughter, a hammered finger, a simple sandwich and cool water on a hot day. To top it off, I remember two-year-old Donna who played in the dirt with my ten-year-old daughter and shared lunch with her mother inside the four snug walls of their new home while her dad, through tears, expressed his gratitude.

That building is precious to me because of what was invested to make it happen.

Likewise, the investment in purity for my marriage was purchased with a hefty price. Years of self-denial and memories of tears when I would *not* get a call from a guy I liked because he realized I wouldn't "put out" and, eventually, clenched jaws as Mark and I chose over and over to say goodnight—to wait—when what we wanted was to go for it—have made our sex life a strong tower we built together, stone by precious stone.

> In college, I was busy with trying to support myself through school and getting a music degree which meant every spare minute was practicing and learning my craft on multiple instruments. The girlfriends I did have, I really had no business having. There was just no time. I guess that was one of the benefits of my chosen degree.
>
> **WONDER-HUBBY MARK**

Even now, many years later, the tearing down of marital fidelity would come at too great a price. Those years of delayed gratification continue to light an extra spark between us with so many memories of *not* removing clothing, etc. Our lovemaking is a priceless treasure that continues to build in value.

Denying yourself and setting boundaries sounds pretty constricting, eh? However, think of it as the narrow gorge you must pass through in order to gain access to a wide, fertile valley—a place of mutual trust and a deep, treasured bond that gets stronger and more fulfilling as the years go by.

Like the little pig who chose to build with bricks instead of straw, investing sexual responsibility in your future takes more work as you lay a foundation of prayer, delayed gratification, sacrifice, and WAITING—but marriage built on that foundation has built-in strength to face life's storms.

It's not possible to live in a bubble, to never see or hear enticements to hop in bed before marriage, but there's a better solution than spending all your time and energy trying to hide from that great big, sinful world.

DEVELOP AN ADDICTION FOR SOMETHING MUCH MORE FULFILLING

Gourmet Love—Sex that Thrills, Fulfills & Heals

I mean, Mickey D's is okay in its place—like, when I'm starving and there's no prospect of something better down the road.

But, if you tell me there's a feast ahead of fresh, ripe strawberries, roast chicken so moist it'll fall off the bone and piping hot homemade bread, crisp and tender, right out of the oven with lots of real butter, and an endless array of gorgeous veggies cooked to perfection, and hot, fudgy brownies with a big vat of home-churned ice cream, I'll blaze by Mickey D's without giving fat-soaked fries a second thought.

Sex can be that feast for you that never ends, bonding in a deep, lasting, satisfying way, fulfilling your hunger for intimate connection with the most important flesh-and-blood person in your world. If you choose not to settle for the cheap, fast fix but rather invest in protecting and preserving your treasure of physical expression for your lifetime mate, a lifetime of sex the way it was meant to be—sex that thrills, fulfills and heals—*can* be your ongoing reward.

Keep your Mickey D's. I'll wait for the feast.

CHAPTER 13

THE GOAL

"If you aim at nothing, you'll hit it every time."
ZIG ZIGLAR

Have you ever wanted anything with such intensity, you were willing to do anything, change anything, sacrifice anything that would stand in the way of that goal? I found myself in that position as a young mom.

We had a toddler son whom we adored and my hubby and I were thrilled when we discovered we were once more expecting. Problem was, at about ten weeks, I had a miscarriage.

"These things just happen," stated the doctor. "Try again."

So we did. Again we were pregnant. Again we went through short-lived joy only to experience the same heartbreak.

Suddenly, my faith felt like a disintegrating raft in a hurricane. Where was God? Why did my body fail me? Why didn't my prayers "work?" Why was I holding a plastic storage bag with a little polyp that had been the baby growing inside? That two-inch piece of flesh represented my heart—detached, cold, and lifeless.

If ever I felt like a graveyard, that was the moment. My hopes and dreams were dead.

But thank God that wasn't the end. Looking back I can see it was a new beginning. I was so broken I was ready for a completely new viewpoint regarding health, one that might even involve (gasp!) *change*. And an even more foreign concept for this sugarholic, I was ready to embrace *self-discipline*.

But first I needed wisdom. Since the regular medical establishment at my disposal offered nothing of substance beyond sympathy, I cast my lot with an alternative doctor in the area who already had the trust of several of my friends. Pride was gone. I was ready to *learn*. I had discovered a goal that eclipsed the momentary satisfaction of hot cookies and brownies. My focus was reborn. Milk shakes were replaced by vitamin-rich protein shakes and green became a color of food served at every meal, because momentary desires were *nothing* when compared to the goal of holding a healthy newborn in my arms.

I was willing to pay whatever price it took, deny my sweet tooth over and over, because, when added together, those choices aimed toward new life. Drink something that tastes like swamp water? No biggie—*if* it fits the plan for a healthier me that results in a healthy baby.

The horrible experience of miscarriages gave me the gift of laser focus. Where I had been lazy for three decades concerning nutrition, (and content to remain so) I now had a backbone of steel because I had a goal that *eclipsed momentary gratification.*

Hopefully you're not as hardheaded about your sex life as I was about my health. It will be so much easier if you don't have to go through horrible circumstances to wake up to what truly counts in life. If you can be convinced to guard your sexual intimacy until marriage, you can avoid a world of hurt, instead of having to hit a wall of despair—perhaps even a life-and-death crisis—to wake up to the fact that "safe sex" outside of a lifetime commitment is a lie. But life is seldom that simple and many of us have to smash into a dead end before we'll admit we're heading in the wrong direction.

But, regardless of your experiences, whether joyful or devastating, I pray this is a chance for you to rise above current sexual trends to see truth and a goal that *eclipses immediate gratification.*

Let's be introspective here.

INTROSPECTION: SELF-ANALYSIS, SELF-EXAMINATION, SOUL-SEARCHING

- For what dream are you willing to change?
- What is bigger than your immediate gratification?

Is there anything? Or are you at the mercy of "I want what I want and I want it now?"

Are you brave enough to stop the runaway train of your life long enough to see if it's heading off a cliff?

Are you foolish enough to believe for something better? Perhaps a great love that lasts a lifetime?

Join me in peering through a future spyglass for a glimpse of what could be in your future, if you have the guts to dream big and stay on course.

Imagine a lifelong relationship that's based on mutual interests and friendship. A relationship where unselfish love is the driving force—so much so that:

- You desire to be a better person
- You desire your mate's happiness even more than your own
- Your focus is on helping your loved one fulfill their highest potential
- You hardly notice that, as you give unselfishly, your own fulfillment is the result
- Over time, the mutual trust and deep bond create a depth of communication that often makes words unnecessary since you are so in tune with the other's moods and preferences

Along with this spiritual and mental connection is an overwhelming desire to meld your bodies, to express physically what is happening in your relationship. But you both want what's best for the other, the most positive and amazing first sexual experience ever. Thus, you agree together to put off sexual expression until there is absolutely no doubt that this relationship *is* forever. And you choose the most powerful springboard into your future; no less than a public declaration of sacred vows before God, family, and friends; the most binding words and action, legally and spiritually, two people can take.

As you witness your partner's unselfish sacrifice of ease and comfort for a higher goal, your respect for each other grows along with this comforting thought, "They will stick by me, no matter what." In turn, the love you thought was as deep as possible, goes deeper still, and the desire for sexual expression becomes a gnawing need.

Still, you stay the course. Just a few more weeks and you'll have the rest of your lives to explore sexuality. You've come this far and gotten so close to your goal, no way will you sacrifice a strong foundation for momentary gratification, a selfish move that will inject regret into your relationship. Therefore you tighten the boundaries, perhaps even cut kisses short and arrange for more time with family or friends in order to avoid breaking this vow to your best friend.

You never dreamed sexual attraction could be so strong. It has become, not just a physical desire, but a spiritual, physical, and mental *need*, the logical progression and expression of two lives melding into one. You can't wait to experience sexual fulfillment together. But you do. You wait. And wait. And the tension builds as the weeks turn into days, and the days become hours, and the last hours turn into a blur of one of the most pivotal experiences of your life. Your two lives become one, joined in a public ceremony that makes official what you have felt for months. "Me" has now become "Us."

Your first intimate sexual experience is freeing, beautiful and pure, with no ghosts of lovers past to inject bitter into the sweet. As the years go by, the sexual intimacy between you is the Holy of Holies[11] of your relationship, the place where what is truly important is brought back into focus, where you recall the excitement and passion of your honeymoon, where you remind each other the wait was so worthwhile and you'd marry them all over again.

What prayer is for the spiritually devout, that's what sex is for a healthy relationship. There are no barriers between you, the individual is lost in the union, and the priority of "us" is reestablished. Sex is where petty disagreements are seen for what they are—petty. Sex is where the bond is strengthened that builds a wall of defense around your relationship,

---

11   Holy of Holies: The innermost chamber of the Jewish Tabernacle. A place regarded as most sacred.

like a high frequency net that drives out even an unseen, underground infestation.

Human sexual intimacy is no less than the treasure chamber of our self-worth. There is no more effective way to undermine the joy and strength of life than to set off a nuclear bomb in the core of someone's soul. The radioactive repercussions, unless intense healing and therapy are applied, continue to devour one's ability to achieve true intimacy and relational health. And the disease is contagious, passed on from generation to generation, destroying a child's faith in lifelong love long before puberty, convincing that child the best they can hope for is "love as long as we feel like it."

No wonder there's so little faith in marriage these days. It's hard to believe in what seems as rare and random as unearthing a priceless diamond in a trash heap. I used to feel the same way when I had lived almost a quarter of a century and had only seen truly happy, lifelong relationships in fiction.

But when I *did* witness a real-life, joyful, deeply-in-love-after-several-decades marriage, it was enough to convince me:

I want a *great* marriage, or no marriage at all.

The rest of the story concerning our quest for a healthy baby through a healthier lifestyle? Within six weeks the alternative doc gave us the go-ahead and we conceived. Not one scary episode occurred during the pregnancy. Nine months later, our baby girl was born, a healthy and beautiful conclusion to one of the darkest moments of our lives. In fact, within four years, two more healthy babies were born and we had all kinds of new challenges to drive us to our knees and force us to grow.

So what will it take to motivate you? A surprise pregnancy or raging STD? A spouse who beats you up and tries to do the same to your kids? An abortion?

Or are you savvy enough to recognize an epidemic and do what it takes to avoid the disease without having to go through hell to wise up?

There is a narrow way that seems unattractive. At first glance it seems restrictive and hard. God is not trying to constrict you. He's trying to save you from broken hearts, despair, betrayal, disease, and a lifetime of regret.

Are you tough enough to buck the system, torpedo your pride and sign up for a boot camp while your friends go out to play?

You'll be made to feel like a freak. You'll be laughed at. You'll be told it's impossible or even unhealthy. (Ha! Right!) You'll have to turn down sexy individuals who are drawn to "the challenge." You'll have lonely, dateless Friday and Saturday nights. And all these factors (and more) will chip away at the good reasons you took the hard path. But let's look down the road of your "harder" choices.

As the years go by, your rewards of healthy relationships, secure children, sweet sleep, burgeoning opportunities, thriving health, and a multitude of other factors will grow, while those around you who took the easy path will build a backlog of brokenness and pain. Or maybe, just maybe, your example helped to encourage others to aim higher.

CHAPTER 14

SEXTERNAL PRESSURES

The best of intentions aren't enough.

Vows aren't enough.

Even prayer is not enough.

Unless your words, goals, and convictions bring about a change in what you DO, they're all empty.

My children took courses in martial arts where they learned to respond with lightning speed if attacked. No, they didn't loiter in dark alleys hoping for an opportunity to use their skills, but if their life was threatened or, God forbid, someone broke into our home, hopefully those survival skills would kick in.

But the time to think, "Gee, I want to know how to defend myself," is *not* when a bad guy has you pinned.

In the same way, if I had waited until things got hot and heavy with my first steady boyfriend to think, "Gee, I wonder if going all the way is such a good idea?" very soon that question would have been moot. Thankfully, I had about four years from the time I received good sexual self-control advice until I needed to put it into practice.

So let's discuss some crucial factors:

- **Who is Dateable**
- **Friends**
- **Intimacy Boundaries**

All these factors and more must be considered and decisions made *before* the fact. THAT'S your plan. Then, to see that plan come to pass, you must keep God first in those priorities.

1. Who is Dateable: Make a list BEFORE you hit the market

Many of us are much more practical when choosing a house or a car than we are about the person we choose to bond with sexually—a decision that, even if that person is not the one we marry, can, with subsequent emotional baggage, make our future home either heaven or hell.

We're like someone looking for a home who says, "But I just can't help myself! That flood plain at the foot of the leaky dam is so exciting! I can't resist!"

Insane, right? But that's what we're doing when we ignore statistics, warning signs, all conventional wisdom, and God's direction when it comes to choosing who we'll date, how we'll date, how we will handle sexual choices and, in some cases, even who we'll marry.

Top of the list of stupid sayings that make me want to spit:

"You can't choose who you fall in love with."

That phrase is code for, "We're just slaves to instinct and emotions. Whoever's the first to respond when our genitals stand up and take notice, that's the person we're stuck with come hell or high water."

What a load of fatalistic crap!

I'll be the first to agree emotions are fickle things. When I was young, a pair of tight jeans on an athletic derriere was hard to ignore. And if that derriere was attached to a guy who made me feel special and desired, well, it was easy to fall for him. But did that mean I should ignore the warning signs and follow emotion to a hot and heavy fling that bound me body and soul to that person?

Sure, emotions are involved in great relationships but that doesn't mean finding love should require a lobotomy. It is, however, an opportunity to force emotions into their proper place—BEHIND God's wisdom.

When I was about twenty-two, I wrote out a list of characteristics for my future husband. In some ways I felt like the kid on Santa's knee who flicks out a list about three feet long. Was I being presumptuous? Was I sounding spoiled? Was it really possible there was a guy on this planet crazy in love with God *and* perfectly suited for me?

Here's a peek at that list.

WHAT I'M LOOKING FOR IN A HUSBAND

1. He will, first and foremost, be "A man after God's own heart" (like King David minus the Bathsheba thing)
2. His love for God will melt my heart
3. He will be extremely attractive to me

> 4. *He will have a good relationship with his family*
> 5. *He will have a deep love for music*
> 6. *He will be athletic—a fun "playmate"*
> 7. *We will have such a deep connection it will almost seem we "read each other's mind"*
> 8. *He will have a great sense of humor*

The list went on with other details like how he would be a great father and would have love for animals too. As I wrote, one more request was niggling at the back of my brain but, honestly, to ask for it was a real stretch of faith.

Finally, even as I struggled with my concept of just how big God is and if, just maybe, this request was judgmental or naïve, I went ahead and wrote:

> *And is it too much to ask, since I've been trying so hard to remain a virgin for him, that my future husband would be a virgin on our wedding night as well?*

There. I wrote it. It was just between God and me and, if it ended up being too much to ask, I could just burn it, right?

But I wrote down my dreams and tucked the list away. When I came across that journal a couple years later, I was shocked by how perfectly Mark, my future husband, fit every request—and even exceeded some.

The fact that I was already very good friends with Mark before we ever had an official date was a healthy circumstance because I had a chance to get to know Mark, his true character, without the tunnel vision of physical intimacy.

Think of it as getting an aerial view of a piece of property before choosing to purchase. If I'm stomping through hills and valleys and deciding this is the place for me because it gives me a "good vibe," has a nice stream and a few pretty flowers but I'm not standing back enough to realize the chunk of land is in a flood zone and sits on a landfill, I don't have a good perspective for making a wise decision.

It can't be denied that physical attraction is a key component for a satisfying relationship but, if such an important decision is based solely on that requirement, you may find yourself bound body, mind, and spirit to a person who is selfish, weak-willed, or even abusive.

THE DATEABLE LIST

So, if you're serious about living out God's best for marriage, get out your trusty pencil and paper to make your own list. Here are some possible details to investigate.

- **Is God first in their lives?**
- **Do they have a rocky romantic past—or present?**
- **Do they have healthy ambitions regarding work, education, and driving passions?**
- **Do they exhibit self-control in their emotions and habits?**
- **Are they a "good influence?"**

How will you know? There's an old saying, "The proof is in the pudding." Do a little detective work before you get emotionally attached.

Who are their friends?

Do they already have a "significant other?"

How do they spend their time?

Do they have a reputation—either good or bad?

How's the relationship with their family?

How do they treat those in authority over them?

How do they treat those in service to them—the waitress, their employees, their pets, their parents, their kids if they have them? If they're in the habit of taking folks who serve them for granted, someday that might be *you*.

One of the many things I love about Mark is that I enjoy him in any setting, whether we're at a party, going out to dinner, getting acquainted with strangers, wrangling family in a hectic airport, or just hanging around the house in sweats. I can rely on him, trust him, and he's never lost the ability to make me laugh—especially at myself. It's the many little character qualities that make entwining my life with his enjoyable.

Best-case scenario: go on group outings rather than plunging immediately into one-on-one to see who they are outside of a dating relationship. As stated before, you get a much clearer picture of their character when you take a bird's eye view of their life rather than just following the thrill of "Hey! They like me! I can't believe it!" and diving into the temporary insanity of too-close-too-soon.

After taking a good, hard look at their character, take out your list of what you're looking for in a potential mate and attach it beneath number one's "God is First in Their Lives."

Does your dream mate hike Mt. Everest with you? Then don't get hooked on Mr, Couch-Potato/Computer-Game Junkie. Is traveling the world high on your list? Look for someone who isn't afraid to color outside the lines. Do you have a desire to feed the poor and buck the "me" generation's selfishness? Miss/Mr. Fashion-Plate-Name-Brand-Everything might not fit the picture.

In other words, use common sense and then pray—a lot! Don't come across as a judgemental prude, but rather stay moldable in God's hand.

He might surprise your socks off by bringing along someone that breaks the mold or by revealing that a close friend of the opposite sex is right for you and they've been hiding in plain sight for years. He might even delay fulfilling your desire for "the one" because other things need to happen first.

FRIENDS

Regarding those friends with whom you might go on group outings, please use sound judgment. As my former ATEAM[12] pal Mark Fortier used to say, "Going out with a couple who is gonna get busy on the table at Buca di Beppo won't help you."

Please choose close friends who will encourage your choices aimed at a healthy, God-centered life. Sure you want to *encourage* those who may be making dangerous choices, but your closest confidantes, the ones you *listen to*, need to be like-minded and have similar goals.

As Victoria Jackson related earlier, when she immersed herself in friends and situations where casual sex, drinking, drugs and the like were no big deal, those things began to look less and less like a big deal to her as well.

INTIMACY BOUNDARIES

Where do you draw the line? For some, that line may be not being alone or choosing to be "alone in public only." For others, it's no kissing. The point is, draw the line where you know sanity is still in charge rather than raging hormones.

---

12   ATEAM stands for Abstinence Through Education And Mentoring. The ATEAM taught the facts about Sexually Transmitted Disease as well as the social, relational, & emotional effects of sexual irresponsibility since unplanned pregnancy is only one aspect.

For my hubby Mark and I during our dating, the boundaries were:

1. Kissing above the neck only
2. No Petting (hands off the bathing suit zone)

Trust me, there was still plenty of opportunity to be lovey-dovey (just ask those friends who probably got nauseous around us in those early, heady days of new love).

So set a healthy, simple standard and stick to it. If there is a difference of opinion, sharpen those communication skills and talk it through. Believe me, honest, thoughtful communication is a great building block for a healthy, long-term relationship.

This whole chapter can be summed up this way: choose daily to stay rooted and grounded in Christ and leave the matchmaking up to Him.

Remember: *"Seek first the kingdom of God and His righteousness and all these things shall be added unto you."* Matt. 6:33 (KJV)

Run all-out toward the center of God's heart and, someday, if you look beside you to realize someone is keeping stride while remaining focused on the same goal, you just might have found the love of your life.

CHAPTER 15

ON MODESTY

Now you're ready to set out on the grand quest of "Save Sex Until Marriage." You brush every shiny hair into place, throw on some magazine-worthy make-up and reach for your favorite outfit, the one that's skin-tight here and plunging there and shows off whatcha got. It's the outfit that makes you feel powerful and turns heads when you walk in a room.

Hold it!

You're not even off the starting blocks and already you're shooting yourself in the foot.

Let's cover some basics.

GUYS ARE VERY VISUALLY STIMULATED.

I would provide tons of scientific data to back up that statement and pages of pithy quotes from psychologists, famous pastors and the like to convince you but it would only bore you to sleep when two simple words will suffice:

PORN. INDUSTRY.

It's a multi-billion-dollar cancer that's sucked down like mother's milk through television, the internet, the printed page, and avenues I'd probably never wish to discover. Selling sex is huge.

To compound this problem, **women long to be desired**. Again, let's skip the scientific explanations of government-funded research and point to the facts. What are the most profitable industries aimed at females?

- **Fashion**
- **Hair care**
- **Skin care**
- **Cosmetics**
- **Weight control**
- **Plastic surgery**

It's all about the next amazing breakthrough that's going to boost our worth, i.e., our attractiveness quotient.

Susie Orbach, psychotherapist and author of the book *Fat is a Feminist Issue* says body image is an even greater problem than she could have imagined when she first wrote her book in the 1970s. The therapist who once treated Princess Diana says girls as young as six are being conditioned to think about cosmetic surgery.

ON MODESTY

Call it the encoding in our DNA that helps to ensure the survival of the species. Those desires are fine when kept in check but, unfortunately, when lust and the need to be desired run amuck, hearts break, families disintegrate, and lives are shattered.

> Some girls may truly not understand what they are doing to guys. They may truly not want to be viewed as cheap. Please understand I never think it's okay to think a girl is "asking for it" by how she dresses. But there are guys who may assume that's what she's advertising.
>
> WONDER-HUBBY MARK

SO… Don't dress like a sex object

While the reaction you're trying to elicit with wardrobe choices is key, there are a few guidelines you should keep in mind since what's considered "sexy" in some geographic locales would be downright vulgar in others. So ladies, fads and acceptable runway attire aside, here are some common sense tips.

1. **Keep Undergarments <u>Under</u>:** Camisoles, slips, bras and panties can be colorful and fashionable but taking your cues for what's acceptability from the Victoria's Secret Runway is a bad idea if sexual responsibility is your aim.

2. **Wear Sufficient Undergarments:** If guys are having a hard time looking you in the eye because your "headlights" are distracting them, get a thicker bra.

3. **WEAR Undergarments:** Guys have a thing for boobs. Deal with that fact and keep yours battened down. Having a nice shape is one thing but making them appear easily accessible says, "Come and get it."

4. **Modest Is Hottest:** If the areas a guy would utilize to impregnate you are in danger of exposure with the slightest movement, the shorts or skirt are too short. Famous pop stars sell more music when they make people stare. Are you selling? And think about it. How many people do you really want to be in on every single, intimate figure flaw? It's none of their business.

There's a lot of talk about undergarments here. Point is, if you're planning to keep your clothes on then… ***plan*** *to keep your clothes on.*

There's a very funny moment in a movie called *Return to Me* where Minnie Driver's character is about to go out with a special guy and her best friend tells her, "Don't shave your legs, then you'll know things won't go too far. Hairy legs may be your only link to reality."

There's more practical wisdom in that statement than we want to admit.

I recall my pre-marriage lingerie. Every now and then I would shell out the big bucks for another pack of white "Jockey for Her" undies and a couple more "jog bras"—you know the type—hooks in the front, has a racer style back and is made for function not display.

That lovely lingerie had no place in the fantasies of my first sexual encounter. I had no desire for anyone to view me in those items. I did not plan for there to *be* any sexual encounters, therefore I dressed accordingly.

Don't get me wrong. I GREATLY anticipated the post-marriage day I would have lacy panties, bras and daring teddies but at eighteen with the newfound freedom of college life and my first steady boyfriend, push-up bras and thong undies were not the way to go.

Again, what you *intend* and what you *communicate* with your clothing choices need to be in line.

ON MODESTY

> I have a good imagination. I don't need the help of more visual aid. And I definitely don't need the inspiration to think thoughts that I shouldn't.
>
> WONDER-HUBBY MARK

As a model in my late teens I started working "market" where buyers would come to view the clothing lines on live models. I ended up securing employment from a high-end company that specialized in fancy gowns and robes, the sort of stuff that's fluffy and lacy but essentially as modest as most prom gowns. The employers were very gracious and assured me I never had to model anything that made me uncomfortable.

Everything was fine until one day I looked out the glass of our showroom to see a couple young men on break from work enjoying our "modeling" a great deal.

While the gowns were modest enough, where would a guy's mind naturally go when he sees a young woman removing the satin robe covering a nightgown? It was a particular way I didn't want to present myself for a man's eyes until it was for my husband on our wedding night.

I quit.

As I knew would happen, it was no problem to find someone to take my place. There were other ways to obtain college money without cheapening something precious.

I never regretted that decision, especially when it was time to remove a robe for my hubby on our wedding night. It was special—for his eyes only—the way it should be.

Now ladies, I realize that some minds in the world are so far gone any woman, regardless if dressed in a burlap sack or a short skirt, would be undressed in the depths of that twisted mind. There are certain things you can't control. However, you *can* control the image you choose to project.

I'm not advocating the latest in fashionable burlap, but please do your part to give the poor guys a break.

Here's the question to ask when choosing the day's attire:

What's my goal:

    a. To present myself as a confident human being who wants to bring out the best in other people?

    OR

    b. To make men's pants get tighter when I walk by?

Bottom line: *What's on the throne?* Is pleasing God your North Star or are you ruled by a deep emptiness, convinced inside that, beyond physical attraction, you're worthless?

Ouch!

I hate to sound redundant but only God can fill that emptiness. Running after the opposite sex to complete you will have the *opposite* effect: sucked dry of self-worth and self-respect.

Again, aim for the center of God's heart with every thought and action and there won't be a need for policing cleavage or skirt lengths.

WHAT MOTIVATES AN EXHIBITIONIST?

We've all heard the stories of someone who gets their kicks wearing a trench coat and flashing strangers. I can only assume the person in question must have such a low self-worth they will do anything to get a reaction from people. What power, to freak people out and tattoo an image on their brains they'll never forget. Hollywood producers spend millions to accomplish that feat.

What motivates this behavior? Perhaps abuse, disdain for the human race in general, or just a misguided need for an adrenalin rush? A multitude of factors contribute to twisted behavior the thrill of which can become as addictive as drugs.

Ladies, are you an exhibitionist, addicted to the adrenalin rush, the power, of turning men on? Do you get a thrill out of your little game of peek-a-boob? Does it back up your general opinion that men are pigs to flaunt their weakness?

Is it their weakness or yours if you feel off balance unless every man in sight wants your body? Again, an addiction requires professional help, and in this case, when there's a gaping black hole of insignificance sucking you toward indiscretion, there's only one source to fill that need—God.

And guys, women aren't alone in this. How tight—or how low—do those jeans really need to be? Maintaining a healthy, vibrant body is one thing, but are you really wanting people to look you over with sex on the brain? Does a deep insecurity drive you to inspire lust?

Once again, only God can fill that black hole of emotional need.

Let's take the issue to God.

Father, you see the emptiness inside of me that needs to have approval and attention. I ask You to fill up the insecurity that constantly seeks validation from other people. Please fill me up with Your love so much that I approach life from a place of overflowing identity as Your precious child with my feet planted firmly on You, the foundation that will never let me down.

In Jesus' name, Amen

I love seeing women dressed up when they feel like a million bucks. When you see that, you see confidence, etc. I appreciate the effort and some occasions call for a very nice evening gown or cocktail dress that may come across as a bit provocative; more fitted, cut a bit more daring, etc. In context, like at an awards show, everyone is dressed like this, like a big, grown-up prom. Basically, I love to see people feel good about themselves, dressed to feel good in their own skin. We've been to a dozen of these events over the years and I know Chana loves getting dolled up.

On the other hand, there are times when you're out and you see someone and you can tell by the vibe that they are projecting a statement—which is: **I need you to think I'm sexy. I need you to think I'm hot.**

I'm more of a "girl-next-door" kinda guy. The vixen-type never appealed to me.

WONDER-HUBBY MARK

CHAPTER 16

A PURPOSE-FULL LIFESTYLE

Be aware of everything around you. Some things strengthen your relationship with God and your sense of self-worth while others undermine it like termites eating away at a home's foundation. Take a long hard look at every aspect of your life including (but certainly not limited to):

1. What you put in your mouth
2. What you put in your ears
3. What you suck in through your eyes

These are some of those moment-by-moment choices where you either cooperate *with* God or prove that His pleasure *is not* the center of your life.

Which item(s) in the following list make your defenses rise?

- That favorite racy television series or movie
- A junk food addiction
- Bitterness and/or hatred for a particular person or race
- Juicy gossip
- Music that fosters your rebellious and/or promiscuous side
- Animosity toward those in authority over you

Yeah, I know. You're looking at this list and thinking, "I knew it! She's getting all *religious* on me." Not in the least. To truly submit yourself to God you lay EVERYTHING before Him. If you can't give Him your choice of music, how will you submit something as personal as your sex life?

Now I'm gonna step on some toes here but, especially in those hormone-charged teen years, what you choose to feed your mind is vital. Think of it like training for the Olympics. An Olympian won't pig out at the ice cream counter or fast food restaurant. That's okay for others, but a competitive athlete has got to consider that one hundredth of a second that will determine victory or defeat.

Still think it's too "religious" to be concerned about stuff like music, movies and TV? Trust me, what runs through your mind directs what you *do*.

One of the most difficult moments of choosing to steer away from pre-marital sex happened when my college boyfriend and I watched a movie called *Making Love*. Go figure. Ironically, I was supposed to review it for a film criticism class. In hindsight, if I'd known what I know now, I'd have opted to fudge the review by reading a few famous critics' opinions. The film wasn't even graphic. But the attitudes, actions, and philosophy of the main characters (who were, of course, gorgeous) were a battering ram to sexual standards. Summary of that philosophy: "If it feels good, don't deny your true nature. *Do it.*"

Hello. Cold shower ahead.

Picture a medieval castle surrounded by thick walls. The enemy is seeking a way in. If they find a weak place in the wall they will chip away at that spot until the wall is breached.

Think about the armor knights wore in battle. Adversaries would study their enemy's armor and aim for the most vulnerable spot—at the neck between the breastplate and helmet or under the arm, for example. That's how you defeat a foe. Aim for their weakness.

Where is the chink in your armor?

- **Stop and take the issue to God.**
- **Shut your eyes and listen.**
- **Write down what He brings to mind.** (Seriously. I'll wait for ya.)

Or, if you're still convinced your armor is impenetrable, go to a straight-talking friend or parent and ask them what they see as your greatest weakness. If you get mad at what they say, they're probably right on track.

Scripture says, *"I have been crucified with Christ. It is no longer I who live but Christ who lives in me."* (Gal. 2:20)

In the story *The Count of Monte Cristo* the hero, Edmond Dantes, saves the life of a pirate by refusing to kill him in a fight to the death. The man whose life Dantes saves proclaims, "I am your man!" From that moment on he lives for the sole purpose of watching Dantes' back and being a devoted, selfless servant.

"You are not your own. You have been bought with a price." (I Cor. 6: 19-20)

Realize what you have been saved from: death, slavery, worthlessness and torment, to name a few. It's as if you were strapped to an electric chair and the switch was about to be flipped but a man came in the room, unfastened the straps, pulled you to your feet, sat in the chair, and requested to die in your place. The act of watching that man's body convulse and die, when it should have been you, would mark you forever.

When you allow it to sink in that it should have been you with the skin flayed from your body hanging on a rough wooden cross gasping for breath as people spit on and curse you, the thought of laying down a few paltry "rights" becomes just that—paltry.

It's all about motivation. Let your choices be governed by your love for Christ and the menial "sacrifices" become a joy.

"I have been crucified with Christ."

That crucifixion includes:

- Your money
- Your future
- Your sex life
- Your friends
- Your body
- Your reputation

DEAD MEN DON'T HAVE RIGHTS.

But according to Romans 12:1, you are a "living sacrifice" so it's a daily choice to leave that stuff in the grave and keep Jesus on the throne. That's where discipline comes in. That's where your daily choices will determine whether or not your life honors God.

- Study the Bible

- Meditate on scripture
- Pray
- Fast
- Give
- Serve
- Spend time with people who go all out for God

These aren't outdated concepts fit only for monks of yesteryear but rather essential tools that mark the difference between a growing, vital relationship with Christ and hypocritical lip service. Jesus said, *"Those who lose their life for my sake will find it."* (Matt. 10:39)

The narrow road is a constant choice but it's motivated by LOVE so the sacrifice results in more FREEDOM that leads to JOY.

Now *that's* a life worth finding.

RECOMMENDED READING:

<u>The Purpose-Driven Life</u> by Rick Warren

CHAPTER 17

HOW NOT TO GO THERE— (SEXUAL PRESERVATION 101)

There was a time in my life when the simple act of finding someone I could be mutually attracted to seemed close to impossible. But add to that Christianity and morality? Ha! I might as well become a nun. It was never gonna happen.

But it was a true test of faith. God had put the desire for a great marriage in my heart so, if I really believed God loved me and wanted the best for me, I needed to believe the unbelievable. Furthermore, I needed to hold that dream with an open hand and make sure God was always on the throne, not my pursuit of Mr. Right.

A funny thing happened on the way to Mr. Right. As I got closer to meeting Mark, I came across a couple "Oh-So-Close-to Mr. Rights." They fit many of the standards, they were Christians, and I was physically attracted to them. But if I had hopped in the sack when I believed "Finally! This is the one!" I would have made a grave mistake.

The basic dating rules became even more essential. Yes, I was past the dangerous teen years but, in all honesty, the fight only got harder as I got older and acquired more freedom. By this time the guys I dated, even though they professed Christianity, had a track record of getting more out of a girlfriend than I was willing to deliver. It was a painful but very telling test of character to see a guy's reaction when his advances were blocked. But did I really want to move closer to marriage with someone who dumped God's standards in private? No.

> The fact that someone "believes in God" or even "attends church" is a good place to start. But if that's the only evidence of God's presence in their life, if they're not drawing you closer to God but enticing you away from God's standards, get out of it. That fact won't magically correct itself when rings are exchanged. If anything, the chasm will only widen. Believe me, marriage doesn't need built-in roadblocks.

With a Higher Standard in mind, we need a plan. Here are a few key factors to help you preserve sexual integrity in an over-sexed world.

MEET THE FAMILY

One of my favorite moments in the movie *Clueless* is when the daughter's date for the night—a studly, cocky young man—meets her father. The girl's dad looks the kid over and declares these immortal words: "I have a forty-five and a shovel and I doubt anyone will miss you."

When a date meets your family, the not so subtle message is, "We were here first. We love this person more than you can understand. This is where they belong. If anything goes wrong, you'll have to answer to us."

This process is often embarrassing and most teens would rather skip it altogether but, with God's standards as your goal, you're gonna need all the help you can get. There's a reason God established the nuclear family. There's safety in numbers. Biblically, when a family had lots of kids, it meant they had a built-in army when enemies came to call. Your family may drive you crazy on occasion, but in a hard, cruel world that wants to make you feel insignificant and disposable, your family will be the equivalent of a beautiful setting for a priceless diamond or a frame for a masterpiece painting. They give security and significance. Face it, even the Mona Lisa, if discarded on Da Vinci's studio floor, might have been overlooked as "just another portrait."

Most of the people you meet are not going to take the time to see your significance. God knows you are unique and priceless and, if you have family (unless they are way-dysfunctional) they are going to value you more than anyone else in the world. They are your frame and your spot on the wall of the Louvre. When a date meets your family, they are forced to realize you are someone's child, someone's sibling. They are getting to borrow the masterpiece from the museum wall for a few hours, but it had darn well better be returned unscathed and on time!

Speaking of "on time"…

SET THAT CURFEW

When I think back on the instances when I was most tempted to chuck virginity and go for it, ninety-nine per cent of those occurred after eleven at night. Why is that?

- When everything is silent, there's nothing else to distract from sexual arousal
- Darkness feeds the delusion of "no one can see—no one will know"
- Comfort level/intimacy with a person increases as hours pass
- Tiredness, like alcohol, lowers inhibitions

That last one alone should clinch it. If you need your wits about you, say for driving, the last thing you need is alcohol—or to be fatigued. Think of sleepiness as taking off your helmet in the middle of battle. You're vulnerable. In fact, you're a sitting duck.

This concept works especially well for the younger set still living at home where Mom and Dad can back up this commitment. However, if you are already on your own, it's still important to set a time and stick with it. Use the dog as your excuse—"I've gotta be back to walk him or he'll pooh on the rug!"—or an unfinished school or work project. Just do it. Let your date know beforehand and use your handy dandy cell phone alarm for a reminder if necessary.

When I was in my early twenties, the guy I was dating at the time was supposed to drop me off at a friend's house at the end of our date. This gal was still living at home and her parents were out of town so, when my date wanted to hang out a while, she told him the house rule of no guys when her parents weren't home. I backed her up on that. It was her parents' house so we were under their rules. My date was a bit miffed and said a couple demeaning things to my friend for still being under her parents' thumb.

I made some disappointing but important discoveries that night.

1. My date could get ugly when he didn't get his way

2. He had a rebellious streak when it came to rules
3. I didn't like being linked to his display of emotional immaturity

Rules have a way of revealing character. This event saved me the trouble of discovering them later when I might have been more emotionally attached.

But having a definite "date over" time is more than just a rule to see how your date reacts to rules. It's another bit of wisdom that could mean the difference between a lovely kiss goodnight or a major groping session. Trust me, your defenses will not strengthen in an open-ended situation where basic fatigue and coziness are taking over.

If your goal is to aim for the direct center of God's heart, you will not dance as close as possible to the cliff's edge. Be smart. Whether in the early stages or well along the road toward permanent commitment, the safety net of a well-laid plan will be your ally.

HALT!

A friend once told us there were certain factors that "set a guy up" when it came to vulnerability towards pornography. Those factors spell out the acronym HALT and stand for:

Hungry

Angry

Lonely

Tired

I have to laugh as I consider how those four adjectives pretty much apply to any teenager at any moment of any day. If those four factors can be the catalyst to entice an otherwise upstanding adult to peruse a pornographic website, how much more tempted will a lonely, angry, tired teenager be to go too far physically with a willing partner?

Just set the stinkin' time and stick with it. The only thing you will miss is the regret of going farther physically than you intended.

SAY "NO THANKS" TO ALCOHOL

> "I have a reputation for a night I don't even remember and the whole school knows."
>
> ~Audrie Potts, 15 year-old who passed out at a party, was sexually assaulted, then cyber bullied with photos of the incident. After writing these words, Audrie committed suicide.

Audrie's story is horrific and heartbreaking. It is even more horrible to realize this is no isolated incident. This agonizing scenario has happened several times in recent years. I cannot begin to imagine the gut-wrenching grief Audrie's parents have endured, the pain of her friends or even the self-hatred, worthlessness, and shame the perpetrators of this crime face every time they look in the mirror. All involved are in desperate need of God's all-absorbing love, grace, forgiveness, and freedom from captivity.

If sexual temptation is so strong we're advised in the Bible to "flee," (I Cor. 6:18) how dangerous is it to drink or otherwise consume something that dulls your senses?

Therefore, if I had to name the one decision that saved me more grief than any other, the choice to avoid alcohol would be it. I was lucky alcohol was not in my home as I grew up. Besides, I could never stand the taste or smell of it. But I, like any teen, *would* have been tempted to fit in with peers. However, some thoughtful adults warned me about how alcohol weakens inhibitions. Thanks to them, I was forearmed. It actually wasn't that hard to maintain. Even when attending parties in college, a soda or cup of water in my hand did the trick and a polite "no thanks" would suffice. But it was heartbreaking at those parties to watch otherwise decent young people acting like morons because alcohol had dimmed their judgment.

Sure I was the target of good-natured teasing and served as the designated driver a few times, but I never regretted missing out on the youthful rite of passage known as a drunken binge and I never woke up in some guy's bed with no memory of getting there. I'm good with that.

On my nineteenth birthday, my college boyfriend took me out for a wonderful dinner (the kind that requires about six waiters just to seat you). Later, after dancing in a revolving restaurant overlooking the Dallas skyline, he wanted to stop for a bottle of expensive wine to celebrate the occasion. I told him I was flattered he wanted to spend that kind of money on me but "no thanks." To his credit, he didn't push the issue and, considering how passionate the kisses were later, it was a good thing I'd turned it down. Adding alcohol to an already sexy evening would have been like pouring gasoline on a flame.

I realize there are locales in the world where alcoholic beverages are an integral, cultural factor. I get that. More power to 'em. All I know is, alcohol mixed with sexual attraction would have been the final nudge to make me say, "Let me at 'im!" on several occasions.

Once again, if your aim is the direct center of God's heart, you'll want to avoid the edge. Wise up! It's a fool who thinks they can buck the statistics and succeed where others fail due to something as avoidable as adult beverages. To revisit the castle scenario, it's like the king decides during war to drop the drawbridge and give the guards a night off. Be smart enough to realize you're just as vulnerable as the young girl giving birth at fifteen, the panicked young man shoving money in her hand for an abortion to "fix" their mistake… or the mortified young lady whose victimized moments are splashed across the internet.

Be honest with yourself, however, and don't try to white-knuckle it through addiction or a family weakness for alcohol or drugs. Lower that pride and GET PROFESSIONAL HELP. It takes a true hero to break the cycle of addiction and start a new tradition of responsible sexual choices and healthy family relationships.

UTILIZE THE "BUDDY SYSTEM"

This one is simple enough. When going out in a non-date setting, have someone trustworthy with you who will watch your back. One young lady related an incident when she was at a dance club. She had ordered soda, but began to feel numb and disoriented. The friends with her got her safely home. She later learned of several instances at that particular club when women had been victimized by the use of a date-rape drug slipped in their drink. Thank God for trustworthy friends!

Audrie Potts' story would have had a much happier ending if she had had a couple watchful, protective friends on hand that fateful night.

To sum up:

1. **Be careful how you dress**
2. **Have your date meet your family**
3. **Set a curfew**
4. **Avoid alcohol and drugs**
5. **Utilize the Buddy System**

CHAPTER 18

AVOID THE "SEXUAL RAPIDS"

The sex act, like getting in the flow of a rushing river, picks up speed the farther you go. How do you avoid getting to that point of no return? Once again, it takes pre-planning and humility to realize you're human and vulnerable. If millions of people down through the ages have fallen over this particular waterfall, there's a reason for it.

IT'S POWERFUL.

Given the right circumstances and a willing partner, you're gonna fall. Add to that a lifetime of misinformation and you'll plunge into that flood early, eager, and ignorant—until you're drowning in heartbreak.

SET YOUR STANDARD

Some lean so far toward caution the couple's first kiss is at the altar when they wed. That would certainly do the trick. For Mark and me, kissing was as far as things went. The "bathing suit" zone was off-limits (no petting) and clothing STAYED ON.

Again:

1. **Kissing is far enough**
2. **The bathing suit zone is off limits**
3. **Keep clothing ON**

There was plenty of room for passion and showing affection, but if we avoided boobs and genitals it was like steering away from the strongest current. Once manual stimulation starts, stemming the tide of sexual urges begins to feel more like turning the Titanic.

Can we just avoid that iceberg altogether?

Even though the discussion of "no sex" may happen, your partner may have other ideas of what's too far. If you feel pressured to go farther physically than you want, say that immortal word "no" and discuss it. If your significant other gets mad or pouts or pulls a guilt trip on you, chalk it up to experience. If they push to get what they want regardless of your desires, it's a major red flag in your relationship. Trust is built or broken in moments like these where one of you says, "No," and the other respects that call. Your significant other's job is to put your well-being ahead of momentary desires and vice versa. As I Corinthians 13 says, **"Love does not insist on its own way."**

When you're aiming for sexual responsibility, you're not pushing *your* desires. You're keeping *God's* desires on the throne. Stick to your guns. Virginity can be quickly lost but not gained back. (although God is *always* into redemption) Guard it like a junkyard dog and be ready for the backlash. Sexual promiscuity has been such an effective weapon in Satan's arsenal, he's not going to let you off the hook without a fight.

Refuse to swallow his rat poison of sweet lies and avoid the devastation to self-worth and future relational and sexual fulfillment.

Therefore, keep the private areas of your body private until you share them with the person who has the guts to stand before God and man proclaiming lifelong commitment to you. They are the one person who has earned access to the treasury and will join you in guarding your marriage with that same commitment.

THE GIRL WHO WAITED

When I met Cassie, she was a woman vibrantly in love. You know the type. She glowed with joy and excitement as she gushed about her fiancée, explaining that she was nineteen when they met. She was the lead in a stage musical and he was a humble member of the chorus. He was a couple years younger than her and totally smitten by the leading lady.

The real twist to the story? Cassie was telling me these details when she was thirty-six years old.

It was fifteen years later that Cassie and her admirer reconnected and began to date. All that time, Cassie had waited, knowing she didn't want to have sex until marriage. "Many times I gave up hope that I would *ever* be married," Cassie said with a roll of her large blue eyes.

When their dating relationship became serious, Cassie made it clear she had waited this long for sex and she darn-sure wasn't going to give up now that it appeared she had discovered her one and only.

Her boyfriend made the adjustment to what he laughingly called "junior high dating rules."

"He was wonderful," Cassie says. "He told me, 'I waited fifteen years. What's a bit longer?'"

Cassie, who held on to virginity for thirty-six years, is now married. Any regrets?

"Not on your life!" she says with a wide grin.

> My dear mom wanted me to know the human facts, so one day when I was stuck home with a cold, she sat on the side of my bed with several library books. She used all correct terminology and was very thorough—much to my embarrassment. I was in 4th grade. Fast forward to my senior year in high school—Advanced Biology had a nine-week period of sex-ed included. I had never had a date and was only friends with the boys. We took a pre-test before beginning the unit and guess who only missed one? Yep—me!
>
> One of the "cool" boys sat in front of me and turned around SHOCKED that I got the highest score on the pre-test! It was pretty funny.
>
> Jean

ON SAFETY: A QUICK GUIDE

1. Always be alert and aware of your surroundings.

2. Use the Buddy System.

3. Learn some basic self-defense.

4. Never get into a car, especially alone, with somebody if you have the slightest prickle of warning in your gut. (Most rapes are committed by acquaintances, not strangers.)

5. Keep Mom and Dad (or another trusted adult) in the loop about where you are and whom you're with at all times.

6. Be okay with it if parents say "No" to your plans or if a trusted friend expresses concern. Their radar may be picking up something yours isn't. In the grand scheme of things, it's highly preferable to endure a boring night than to wind up raped... or dead.

CHAPTER 19
THE VOICES IN YOUR HEAD

"My god, Vanessa's got a smashing body. I bet she can shag like a minx! I hope I didn't say that out loud just now."
AUSTIN POWERS

There's a coach in your head. With every word, every action, you are obeying that internal director. Problem is, no matter what vows you make, if the constant internal monologue pulls you in the opposite direction, you will fail. Time to get a winning coach.

A Cherokee legend explains this concept very well.

> **An old chief tells a young warrior, "There are two wolves battling inside of you. One is good and the other is evil."**

The warrior asks, "Which one will win?"

The wise chief replies, "The one you feed."

What are you feeding your mind? If you view the world as a huge smorgasbord where it's fine to gorge on whatever is most attractive and available, like a five-year-old set loose in a candy store, you'll soon have a flabby, undisciplined, sick mind.

Think of your life as a ship. The wind and waves (circumstances) have influence, but it's the rudder (your tongue) that turns the ship—and the ship's captain turns the rudder.

The surest way to find out who's steering the ship? Note the words. The old adage "garbage in, garbage out" is right on target. Our mind overflows through our mouth to steer our life onto the rocks or, by filling our mind with God's viewpoint, that overflow steers us into vibrant *life*.

Wouldn't it be so much easier if Jesus' white-robed arm was on your shoulder through every decision, feeding you the words to say, warning you away from danger, and even embracing you when things are tough? The disciples had that for three years and, guess what, they still didn't get it. Every day they followed Jesus, had meals with him, watched people get healed, saw Him walk on water, and even raise the dead. But when push came to shove and people wanted to kill Jesus, they all either ran away or acted like they didn't know Him. One of the disciples even set Jesus up for arrest.

Jesus said it was better for us if He *went away*. Why? Because when He went to heaven, He returned in the form of the Holy Spirit to *live inside us* as our teacher, comforter, constant companion, and helper.

In the second chapter of Acts, the New Testament believers waited for this Comforter that Jesus said would give them power to tell people effectively about Him. There were all the believers, hiding together, afraid the Jews or the Romans would burst in and arrest them.

But as they prayed, little flames of fire appeared over their heads and they began to speak in other languages. Soon, other people in the city gathered to check out the commotion and heard the story of Jesus recounted in their own language, by people who didn't speak those languages. Suddenly there were over three thousand new believers in one day!

Yeah, I'd call that power.

The good news is, that same Holy Spirit who visited the disciples and turned ordinary fishermen into spiritual powerhouses, is available to us right now. That's why it was so important that Jesus didn't stay here and whip everything into shape as one perfect king. People only truly change *from the inside out.* When we ask Jesus to take over our lives, He takes up residence in our spirit. He becomes our new coach.

In this way, God is with you 24/7/365, in the best of times, the worst of times, and all those mundane times in between. Much better than a once-in-a-lifetime meeting with Jesus, we have access anytime to God's constant guidance when we learn to be still and get to know His voice. But just like the Native American tale of the two inner wolves, the *one you feed* is the one who will win. We have a moment-by-moment choice to either put Jesus in charge, to obey His guidance… or not.

This is where the things done in secret will begin to show.

Want to know God's voice better?

*Get alone and listen.

Want to have God's outlook on things?

*Study the Bible.

Want to have God's love for people?

*Spend time praying for them.

John the Baptist said it best, "He must increase. I must decrease." (John 3:30)

As you consciously make room for Jesus, your mind will get more and more used to thinking His way.

As an early Christian who had been used to acting a certain way around old friends, I found it difficult to go to school every day and try to act and react by God's guidance rather than habit. Each morning, I would fix a picture in my mind of Jesus entering the school with me, standing beside me during conversations, and looking over my shoulder in class. Over and over I blew it and would look back on the day feeling like a loser.

That visual inner picture was helpful but it was like I was trying to be what I wasn't yet. When I finally understood Christ wasn't just watching, He was *in* me through the Holy Spirit, I began to understand it wasn't about me gritting my teeth in order to be good enough. It was up to Jesus to transform me from the inside out. But I could choose whether I would cooperate with His renovation or get in the way. I constantly had a choice.

MUSIC: YOU ARE WHAT YOU REPEAT

Luckily, in my teen years, Christian music was becoming popular. There were Christian radio stations and a few wonderful artists with songs that stuck in my mind.

But the transition to what I thought of as "Jesus Music" wasn't easy. To be honest, I missed listening to Michael Jackson, Heart, and The Cars to name a few. In fact, the first few months required a tough transition. Music had been my escape. I always enjoyed getting lost in a book but music was a wonderful, quick fix. With one well-placed, catchy beat my mood transformed from the depths of despair to giddy, dancing joy. Therefore, I was a bit like a caffeine addict trying to steer clear of the Starbucks on every corner. But soon the new tunes paid off big time. When? When *life* happened. The death of a loved one, shattering of a dream, betrayal of a friend, or simply a royal fail—those out-of-fashion, "religious" songs were my IV. When I didn't have the energy to pray or quote scripture or even call a friend, I could at least let an uplifting song flow through my mind like the cool, cleansing, refreshing water of a deep well. Sometimes I sang the songs, sometimes a sob was the best I could do but those memorized verses of encouragement and focus on God proved to be a lifeline.

If no one's told you, allow me: Life. Is. Hard. The attack WILL come. Therefore, stuff your mind full of ammunition for the lean times. WHEN you are ambushed (did you really think the devil would fight fair?) God's words, from scriptures and songs that focus on Him, will give strength, hope, peace and faith—you know, all the stuff life sucks away.

FEEDING THE BAD WOLF:

A young adult trying to buck the system and maintain sexual responsibility until the "I do's" is running a marathon. Provocative lyrics and sexy images are more than just "empty calories" for your mind, they are pumping in the exact opposite of what you want to accomplish. Do yourself a favor and work WITH God on this. Do a major spring-cleaning of your musical selections and ask, "Does this please You, God?"

I'm not saying everything on your playlist has to sound like *Amazing Grace* but if indiscriminate sucking down of the latest foul-mouthed, amoral reprobate is your definition of "cool" and you savagely defend your musical selections with the phrase "I listen to it for the music. The words don't affect me," you're living in a fantasy world.

You're in a contest where the stakes are much higher than an Olympic gold medal and your picture on a cereal box. Your decision in the heat of the moment could spell the difference between a close shave or a lifetime of regret.

A good friend of mine wrote about her heartbreak when she perused the songs on her daughter's playlist and had a discussion with her teen about attitudes toward sex in today's culture.

Her daughter told her, "It's not a special, secret thing anymore. Sex is a joke. And it's not 'sex' or 'making love,' it's 'smush, smash, bang, tap, hit.'" She also said that even the kids at her Christian school say the F-word and all the other curse words. They listen to music riddled with b*#ch, ho, f***, hump, etc. "After a while," she said, "we get numb to it."

Her daughter said the first song she loved that had a bad word in it was by the Black-Eyed Peas. "I felt guilty for liking it, so I would sing along but never say the word. But then as time went on... "

Music is a powerful thing. We've all been there. A bad day, a nasty break-up, some major disappointment and then a song meets you right where you are and gives your mood a kick in the pants. Music opens your spirit in ways words alone can't. In the Bible when Moses or Joshua was leading the Israelites into battle, often the musicians led the way.

Get that. The lyre was mightier than the sword.

Were you under the impression the rock god pounding away on a guitar with his skinny body and lank, unwashed hair induced screaming females to toss undergarments at his feet because of his good looks? No. It's an emotional and *spiritual* response—a powerful pull to *worship*.

"Have no other gods before me." *(Ex. 20:3)*

Is music something that plays and replays in your mind even in the silence? Of course. So, what are you sucking down? Are you hooked to an IV of poison that flows through your spirit 24/7? Do you think you can "handle it" without any negative consequences?

WHAT ELSE FEEDS YOUR MIND?

My friend and her daughter, after discussing that music list, made a list of TV shows that push, endorse, or encourage sex outside of marriage. The list got so long they suddenly realized that every TV show, every movie and every song teens hear is a constant chant that says, "Do it, do it, do it, do it."

- **Movies**
- **Television**
- **The Internet**
- **Video Games**
- **Books**
- **Friends**

In every one of these areas (and more) there is a choice to make.

The Bible says our heart is our wellspring. (Prov. 4:23) Are you guarding it or helping to muddy the water?

How's about a new tactic? What if, rather than trying to see how close to the edge you can dance, you aim instead for the dead center of God's best? What if you fill your mind with stuff that's right and pure and honest and true? Let it be a paradigm shift in your focus. Choose what goes into your mind with the single-minded determination of a world-class athlete.

Philippians 4:8 says, "Whatever is true, honest, just, pure, lovely, of good report, virtuous, or praiseworthy, think on these things." Let that be the measuring stick for your mind's fuel. If it doesn't help you aim for the center of God's heart, *drop it.*

Conclusion: If you want something running through your brain besides "Do it, do it, do it," it's going to take a concerted effort.

IF IT'S JUST RELIGION, IT'S CRAP

Just surrounding yourself with all the trimmings of a Christian life won't be enough. Make sure, day-by-day, that God is the One you're aiming to please. Jesus even went so far as to say that other relationships in your life—even family relationships—should look like *hate* when compared to your overwhelming commitment to and love for God. "In *all* your ways acknowledge Him, and He will make your paths straight." (Prov. 3:6)

Paul, who wrote most of the New Testament in the form of letters to the early believers, called it "circumcision of the heart." Rather than just showing our faithfulness to God by staying sexually pure, Jesus asks us to keep our hearts pure by being aware of what we are linking to the Holy Spirit who dwells inside. Jesus went far beyond the Jewish laws, that were impossible to keep to the letter, and asked us to be clean *on the inside.* This impossible feat can only be accomplished by falling so madly in love with Jesus that it breaks your heart to break His. And this mindset only happens as His Holy Spirit works *inside*.

I realize that asking you to be sexually pure in a sexually charged generation seems like an impossible task. Yes, it's tough, but *not* impossible. You are not an animal in heat. Besides, you don't have to go it alone. When God is in you, He promises, "I will *never* leave you or forsake you."

God has never gone back on His word. He will be with you *all the time,* coaching, comforting, guiding, and teaching you His ways. With God in charge—because you put Him there by free will choice—your inner monologue will steer you toward His best for your life.

CHAPTER 20

TRUE LOVE EXERCISES SELF-CONTROL

When I met Mark, he was still in college and I had already graduated so I assumed he was too young for me; although man, was he cute! We hung out with the same crew at church, and we were counselors at a Christian camp in the summer. We worked as leaders with the church's youth group, and threw paper wads at each other over chocolate shakes at Chili's in an ongoing sort of sibling rivalry for close to a year before I finally admitted, "Ohmigosh, I could see myself marrying this guy!"

We'd never dated, certainly never kissed, but I was already well on the way to "in love." By the time we finally did anything one-on-one, we were both so concerned about losing our friendship we wouldn't call it *a date*. After all, if you're open to a new relationship it's because former relationships have crashed and burned. Do ya really wanna risk a great friendship on that?

Also, it was the first time I'd ever stared down the road of dating a person with the fear *I* might screw up and hurt *him*. Wow! That was turning the tables. As Randy Pausch, internet phenomenon and author of the bestseller *The Last Lecture* said about the difference he felt when he was falling in love with his wife—"For the first time, *the other person's happiness mattered more than my own.*"

Let me tell you. All that smart-aleck energy had no trouble turning on a dime into sweetness as we both finally admitted to the world we were a couple. Did it make it easier to not want to go for it? No! The seeds of real love made those rules more essential than ever because we were dealing with much more than mere physical attraction. We shared similar tastes in everything from sports to movies and enjoyed each other so much our mutual temporary poverty mattered not one whit as we opted for pizza and rented movies rather than wining and dining. We'd found where we belonged. The trimmings didn't matter.

Oh, how many times we had to pry ourselves away from each other and call it a night! In some ways I trusted him more than I trusted myself because, as a female connecting spiritually and mentally on such a deep level for the first time, the body wanted desperately to follow suit. I'd never had such a deep connection with anyone. With one look Mark could communicate a private joke that would have me choking on laughter. His ability to make me laugh was coupled with a trusting, beautiful relationship with God that humbled me. He was precious. He was God's. I truly didn't feel worthy. It was a sort of holy fear of coming between him and God that provided the necessary backbone to give his future the best possible foundation even if—horror of horrors—*it wasn't with me.*

We discussed things that were making the commitment of no sex before marriage difficult and even tightened a couple parameters. It was a mutual commitment and, though the topic wasn't always easy to discuss, it was a great foundation of learning to communicate to achieve a common goal. Besides, it served to deepen my respect for Mark because he was able to address problems without becoming defensive—a lesson I'm still trying to learn.

Mark was showing that he was a real man, one who was willing to wrangle the greatest foe of all—himself—to put God first. In the process, we both were learning to love in the healthiest way.

> I had lots of people telling me, "Well, you want to be ready, you want to have sexual experience." I think that's another argument for people trying to justify what they're doing.
>
> WONDER-HUBBY MARK

The movies and television would convince you true passion is something that's overwhelming and undeniable. True, passion IS overwhelming but *there's always a choice.* You can allow lust to be your god or you can shove that heady wine off God's throne and, like a trainer with whip and chair, force it UNDER God's laws.

Allow me to go on a metaphorical binge. Think of all that passion as something you control like the flow of a rushing stream by building a dam that stores those urges and holds back the flood until the proper moment. What has happened now? You have stored up passion for lean years, for those moments when a new baby has sapped your sleep and you need to remember all the nights you chewed up a pillow because you wanted your mate so badly. Passion for when things are financially tough and you both need to be encouraged and recharged by a satisfying sex romp that reminds you what's truly important in life. It's become a storehouse of energy and a deep well of passionate "reserves." Plus, there will be times, even in marriage, when sex won't be an option such as during sickness, right after a baby's birth, or during an unavoidable absence. It's nice to know your mate knows how to be celibate if life forces the issue.

TRUE LOVE EXERCISES SELF-CONTROL

Think of it as training in the fine art of MONOGAMY. You can both look forward, just like you did before marriage, to the moment when you get to release the dam!

Plus, is that young man or woman *really* interested in your highest and best if their immediate sexual release is more important than your future health, family, aspirations, and spiritual well-being? One is momentary. The rest sticks with ya.

Maybe you don't like rules. Maybe you feel it's an insult for someone to think you have this common sexual weakness. Maybe you believe, along with many, that something as beautiful as sexual attraction should not be thwarted. Maybe you believe planning strategies to avoid pre-marital sex will only heighten your fascination with it. Maybe you believe that you and your partner are different, that pre-marital sex will only strengthen your long-term commitment to each other.

Maybe you think you know more about sex than God—the One who created sex in the first place.

THE FOUNDATION FOR EVERYTHING ELSE

Perhaps you're thinking, "Why do you keep harping on my relationship with God? What does that have to do with my sex life?"

The answer? **Every stinkin' thing!**

Think about it. When God pulled Abraham aside and chose a mark for his physical body to signify the future Israelite nation, what did He choose? Did he ask him to cut off a finger to remind his people not to steal? Did He have Abraham pluck out an eye to signify "look upon no evil?"

No. He chose circumcision (an "incision that encircles"). It was a sign on their sexual organ, to remind them He was God of their most secret, intimate practices and, like a wedding ring signifies the unbreakable marital bond, cutting away the foreskin signified they belonged to Almighty God. Circumcision showed that those hidden choices are the ones that set them apart and established the strength—or weakness—of their nation and God's plan of redemption through the promised Messiah.

To trust that God loves you enough even to fulfill your sexual desires takes a lot of faith—especially when you've been told God says sex is wrong. Far from it! Sexual intimacy is a precious gift that, like the crown jewels, requires a high level of security to keep it safe. Screwing up in that area can turn a precious gift into a curse.

It's that awful phrase—**Self Discipline**.

Does self-discipline mean a life minus fun? NO! This is not some legalistic, judgmental thing where you sit in a bubble to protect yourself from a big, sinful world. But, if there are things pulling you over the waterfall right now, you'd better jump! Grab a therapist, a minister, a trusted friend, enroll yourself in a rehab, whatever it takes to *run away from* habits that will wrap a noose around your sexuality, your self-worth, your goals and dreams, and everyone to come in your family tree.

As Dave Ramsey, author of *The Total Money Makeover*, says when he's teaching people how to escape financial slavery: "Choose to live like no one else, so that later you can *live like no one else.*"

It's the same with your sexual choices. When it comes to sexuality, living like no one else begins with *thinking* like no one else.

> It's like a Treasure Chest. From that Treasure Chest you get freedom, you get trust, you get excitement because you've stockpiled all those wants and desires and you get to open them together on your wedding night. Not only is this "okay" now, it's commanded. Whaaat?!
>
> WONDER-HUBBY MARK

DELAYED GRATIFICATION

de-layed adj.—*happening at some time after the usual or expected time*

grat-i-fi-ca-tion n.—*pleasure or satisfaction*

Gratification? No problem. Pleasure and satisfaction are the highest priority in our society. But add the word "Delayed" on the front and suddenly it's a foreign language. We're all about *instant* gratification—fast food, fast cash, instant messages.

Wait is today's dirty, four-letter word.

But please stop and think. If you're aiming for your own Great Love For Life, you will need a deep appreciation for this concept. You owe it to yourself to think through irreversible actions. Your decisions now could result in a healthier, happier, self-respecting you enjoying a home that's a haven. Conversely, those decisions could turn your entire life into a war zone. Will that tumble in the back seat on a Friday night pay off a couple years down the road? Or will it be one step closer to future divorce, heartache, lost dreams, lost health, and self-medication with drugs, alcohol, or sexual perversion to drown your despair?

Sure, it's a free country. No one can deny your right to self-destruct. But there really *is* a choice. You really can aim for hope. Please. Find that reason that's bigger than your sex drive and get your hormones out of the driver's seat before you destroy yourself and those you'll take down with you.

Yeah, I can hear it, the same voices you're hearing in your head right now:

"Those abstinence things never work. People just make vows and then do it anyway."

But here's an opportunity to learn a new way of thinking, a goal worth delaying gratification, tips to help when the rubber meets the road—or when you're tempted to use a rubber thinking it will make devastating choices "safe."

Again, "Choose to live like no one else, so that later you can *live like no one else.*"[13]

> Twenty-five years of NO turns into YES in one day and it's like you're living a dream because there's no guilt, no shame—there's a lot of working it out and laughing—to me that's so much better.
>
> WONDER-HUBBY MARK

---

[13] Find all Dave Ramsey's books and other financial training tools here: daveramsey.com

CHAPTER 21

WHO'S ON FIRST?

There's a song called *You Are Mine* by Mutemath that does a great job spelling out the meaning of priorities.

> *"Everyone has their obsession*
> *Consuming thought, consuming time*
> *They hold high their prized possession*
> *That defines the meaning of their lives*
>
> *You are mine*
> *You are mine*
> *You are mine, all mine*
> *You are mine"*

Read those words again and ask yourself:

1. What consumes my thoughts?

2. What consumes my time?
3. What is my prized possession?
4. What defines the meaning of my life?
    - Career?
    - Romantic pursuits?
    - Food?
    - Computer games?
    - Physical appearance?
    - Financial security?
    - Competitive sports?
    - Selfish pleasure
    - Reputation?
    - Thrill-seeking?
    - Revenge?

And just in case you're still having a hard time being honest with yourself, let's take it a step further.

Someone who made a tremendous impact on my life, Reverend Peter Marshall Jr., defined idolatry as:

> *"Whatever you think about the most, whatever you talk about the most, whatever controls your emotions—that is your god."*

I didn't want to hear it at the time. But that definition made a profound change in the course of my life in my early twenties and still serves to knock me back on course when priorities get out of whack.

So, grab a piece of paper and write down your answer to these three questions:

1. *What do I think about the most?*
2. *What do I talk about the most?*
3. *What controls my emotions?*

Be brutally honest. What/who is the first thing on your mind when you wake? What/who is usually the topic of conversation? What/who do you turn to in a crisis? What/who do you spend your money on? What/who can turn you from calm & collected to raging lunatic in a nanosecond? What/who can turn a happy day into a black hole of despair?

Maybe it seems strange for a discussion about sexual purity to focus on idolatry. But in order to buck the system, you have to make a conscious decision about what is going to be the North Star in your life, your anchor, that thing around which everything else revolves.

Choose carefully or you'll find your self-worth and life's ambition built on something that changes like the phases of the moon—emotions, physical beauty, career, a need to be needed, a need to prove yourself, or even something purely destructive such as revenge, anger, or self-hatred (a tricky form of self-idolatry).

Remember Jesus' parable about the wise man building on the rock and the foolish man building on sand? The storms were unavoidable. The choice for each man was *where and how to build.*

Let's face it. In many ways, life is an ongoing desert and we're all starving for water. You have to decide what you'll suck down when everything turns to blistering heat, a plague of locusts, and blinding sand.

Problem is, if we get used to a shallow source of Orange Crush or straight up poison in the oasis times, it'll be habit to turn to those non-satisfying/destructive things in a drought.

- A rock in the storm
- A deep, clean well of life-giving water in the desert
- The star that helps you find direction

What's yours? What (or who) can fill those needs? What do you do if you realize your foundation is quicksand?

YOUR "GO TO"

What's the hardest addiction to kick you can think of? Food? Smoking? Alcohol? Pornography? Sex? Fame? Power? Heroine? Meth?

That last one, so I've learned, is next to impossible to beat, but Brian "The Head" Welch of Korn fame did it. In his book *Save Me from Myself*, Brian tells the story of his descent into drug addiction and the moment when he gave up—and asked God to heal him.

After that encounter with God, Brian was able to keep his commitment to stay off drugs, and to be a responsible dad to his daughter. With God's help, Brian was able to *change*.

Yes, the task of self-control is difficult, but just like someone who kicks drug addiction, food addiction, pornography, or any other harmful habit, you too could defy the odds. When the goal is firmly in mind, a plan is in place, and God is put in the driver's seat, the impossible becomes, not just possible, but indescribably worth it!

Do you think Brian "The Head" regrets kicking his addiction? No. He's alive today because he did.

It's the same thing with sex. The goal is not just some legalistic rules to take the fun out of your life but rather a decision to aim *for life*—to bypass habits that would kill your future, or even kill *you*.

But be forewarned. Here are just a few of the obstacles standing in the way of you enjoying sexual health God's way:

a. **Cultural prejudice:** We've all heard it "Abstinence doesn't work!" I say you've just never been motivated enough. If you have the mindset of a zebra out-running a hungry lion, you'll do whatever it takes. Yeah, the zebra's got a run for their money, but it happens.

b. **Your sex drive:** All those hormones can make wrangling wild mustangs seem like a stroll in the park.

c. **Negativity from friends or even family:** Misery loves company, mediocrity is contagious, and pulling down is easier than pulling up. When you aim higher, it may be perceived as judgmental.

d. **A mountain of statistics:** Tons of cultural pressure stating that two people coming through this minefield to enjoy a lasting marriage—especially, both never having had sex before—is impossible, or at least impossibly old-fashioned.

e. **The media:** Almost every movie, television program, popular song, internet article, magazine article, novel, etc. entices you to be sexually active. And man do they wrap it purty! Parties and boobs and thrills, oh my!

But look again into the possible ramifications—the teeth of the lion you're escaping when you choose sexual responsibility:

1. Sex equated with shame and fear
2. Bonding with someone and becoming someone who doesn't know how to *stay*
3. Comparing your mate's sexual performance to others
4. Cheapening of the covenant of marriage
5. Less meaning & fulfillment from lovemaking
6. Anger and hatred for self and opposite sex
7. Lost health
8. Regret and shame that grows into marital cancer
9. Your mate is an adversary rather than your haven
10. Lost life opportunities
11. Emotional devastation halts emotional maturity
12. Parenthood equated with resentment, fear, shame, regret, and panic
13. Become a statistic of divorce and single parenthood
14. Kids inherit your hell and pass it on

And we end up with a society numbing the pain with addictions—alcohol, drugs, sex, food, debt, etc. That's not life. That's slavery.

LET'S BREAK THE CYCLE!

CHAPTER 22

LAYING A FOUNDATION

"Every great movement of God
can be traced to a kneeling figure."
D. L. MOODY

I remember the horrific images in February of 2010 after the devastating Haiti earthquake. Thousands of buildings collapsed leaving more than 200-thousand dead and millions more homeless. The death and destruction stunned the world. Later that same month, an earthquake of even greater magnitude hit Chile. While Chile endured widespread devastation, the loss of life when compared to Haiti was much lower. Why?

Scientist Carl Nelson in his article titled, "How to Build an Earthquake Proof Building," has a simple explanation.

> *"The difference in those death tolls comes from building construction and technology. In Haiti, the buildings were constructed quickly and cheaply. Chile, a richer and more industrialized nation, adheres to more stringent building codes."[14]*

A poorly constructed building meant the difference between life and death. Please don't think I'm making light of Haiti's horrific earthquake disaster. But we're foolish indeed if we can't learn something here.

In the above quote, the words "quickly and cheaply" leap out at me. Those words are the perfect descriptors for what we have done to the concept of sex. We're pushed to *quickly* throw away the exclusivity of lovemaking. With every step away from that exclusivity, the act becomes increasingly *cheap*. Today's love building blocks are unreinforced concrete waiting to collapse. A quickly, cheaply constructed love life is a death trap.

Therefore, is it legalistic and "religious" to call for a higher building code? No. It's *wise*.

There was an amazing young couple who became mentors and prayer partners for Mark and me at a critical time in our lives. We had to realize even the most perfectly suited mate couldn't fill every need or correct deep emotional wounds. That was God's territory. The process of prayer opened up the cesspools no one could see that would have been the viper in the grass waiting to strike in a vulnerable moment.

It was one more avenue God used to put our foundation on Him. It also made us accustomed to relying on prayer—together. The prayers with our friends dug a deeper, stronger foundation for our married, lifelong love.

---

14   "Can You Build an Earthquake-proof Building"

The Bible is very clear that *"every good and perfect gift is from above."* (James 1:17) When seeking God's best, lay a solid foundation by seeking *Him*. If He is placed first, as the chief architect of your life, the good and perfect gifts that come your way can remain good and perfect, even growing in value because they will thrive when left in HIS care.

Once again, it's a matter of priorities.

Place God first.

Keep God first in your schedule.

Consider God first in your decisions.

Ask God to put a searchlight on every area of your life to expose pitfalls.

Invite God into your thoughts.

Give God your *relationships*.

Give God your *goals*.

Think about what would please Him in the way you dress, talk, spend your money, entertain yourself, etc.

But do yourself and God a favor and really study His personality, not just the perception of God you might get at church or even through others who profess to love Him.

Read the stories of how Jesus loved people. Look for God's sense of humor in Jesus. Be aware of God's grace toward those who had screwed up. Remind yourself of Jesus' gracious acceptance of outcasts and misfits. He defied convention and refused to be crammed into a religious box. So don't assume your life must fit a cookie-cutter mold. God revels in creativity and wants to hone your particular uniqueness.

Get to know God for yourself, not through secondhand knowledge. He alone can fill that black hole inside. HE will be your have-all-to-end-all. Fall crazy in love with Jesus and you won't be such easy prey for a smooth-talker who would be rat poison in your life. Even for those already married, when we're filled inside with God's love, there won't be a tendency to say, "Gee, I feel like I'm missing something. Maybe *that person* will fulfill me." You know you've already found the true source—Christ in you.

If you skip this bedrock, meaning a fulfilling relationship with your Maker, you'll suck the life out of your relationships by trying to force *people* to fill God's shoes. Great sex is amazing. But great sex is a mere shadow of union with God, of that joyful losing yourself in God's vastness, the unity and fulfillment for which you were created. He's the one healthy addiction.

Keep it straight though. GOD is a healthy addiction—not RELIGION. If your relationship with Him isn't the driving force, religion can become another death trap.

God is the only one who can take your baggage—those emotional scars that would sabotage the good He wants you to experience.

"But seek first the kingdom of God and his righteousness and all these things shall be given to you as well." (Matt. 6:33)

Jesus says winning begins with losing—when you lose your life for His sake, you will find it. (Matt. 10:39)

In a culture obsessed with "self-fulfillment," choosing to lose your identity in Christ sounds like death. It is. But it's a death that leads to life and freedom from those things that would kill you.

As in all good things, a great, lifelong love relationship, including great sex, begins and ends in God.

He created it.

He sustains a thriving relationship.

Only He can open the hidden treasure trove of relational and sexual fulfillment.

KICKSTART YOUR DAY

Set your goal to bring a smile to God's face in all you do.

Jesus made following God as simple as possible—

1. *"Love the Lord your God with all your heart, with all your soul, with all your mind and with all your strength."*

2. *"Love your neighbor as yourself." (Mk. 12: 30-31)*

So as soon as your foggy morning brain registers a thought, here's a good way to start the day:

"Hi, God. I'm yours. Everything I have is yours. This day is yours. Anything You want to tell me?"

Number one priority—God. So plan your day accordingly

a. Set aside a few minutes for a simple Bible study

b. Talk to and listen to Him = Pray

If you hear an audible voice, more power to ya, but usually God communicates through thoughts and through phrases in the Bible that will "jump out at you" as you read. If nothing earthshaking happens, cool, but remain faithful. The important thing is to stick with your commitment whether you feel like it or not. It's great practice for getting your emotions off the throne.

PRAISE

"As a man thinks in his heart, so he is." (Prov. 23:7)

Focus on, magnify, glorify, praise—once again, terms that seem outdated and "churchy" are going to be one of your most powerful weapons on the sexual responsibility battlefield.

The devil knows we are creatures who follow our thoughts. Consider the multi-media bombardment every day that strives to cheapen attitudes toward sex. It's going to take real discipline to turn your mind in another direction, namely toward God, with hunky guys and silicon, airbrushed boobs vying for your attention wherever you look.

This is where those choices in music can either help or hurt. Rather than catchy tunes repeating "Do it. Do it. Do it," the songs in your head can keep your mind on your new healthy addiction: God.

Whatever your taste, explore the options and change the soundtrack in your head from "Do it. Do it. Do it," to one that aims for the center of God's heart.

DEAL WITH INTERNAL SCARS

Throughout this book, perhaps many shameful and hurtful experiences have come to mind. What can we do about that?

Start by carving out a time to be completely alone in a place where you feel safe. Talk to God. Write it down if that helps. Pour out your frustrations. Admit the thrill you feel by being a sex object or the need you have for constant attention.

Ask God to do some deep spiritual surgery on the hidden cesspools of your heart. Were you abused, ignored, used, or rejected? Did you long for a father's love and get anger instead?

> **Confess** the secret things that make you feel ashamed, unlovable, and dirty.
>
> **Choose to Forgive** those who have hurt you, even if it feels impossible to forget.
>
> **Choose to Forgive *Yourself*.** Just say the words, "I forgive myself," whether you feel like it or not, and let God take it from there.

Maybe this process stirs up more than you can handle. That's fine. Go to a trusted pastor or counselor and keep the clean-out process going. For Mark and I, our prayer partners, the young couple I mentioned before, helped this vital process. It's the hidden, shameful things that push our buttons and pull our emotional puppet strings. It's time to cut those strings and let God make a garden out of your emotional landfill. Again, only He can fill that black hole of need.

Prayer, scripture memorization, counseling, a support group, all of the above—whatever it takes, ***get free!***

This is not a journey for the faint of heart. It takes a lot of guts to face your demons and learn a new way of thinking. Unplugging from old thought patterns that run on continuous loop in your brain takes time and perseverance. Memorize scripture, especially those dealing with "take every thought captive" and "have the mind of Christ." Start right now with Romans 12: 2: *"Be not conformed to this world, but be transformed by the **renewing of your mind**, that you may prove what is the will of God, what is good, acceptable and perfect."* (NIV)

Rather than viewing your freedom as just walking out of an unlocked prison door (which is what Christ has done for us) the road to wholeness (holiness) needs to be undertaken more like a man buried alive who is determined to keep digging away until he is finally able to push through to breathe fresh air.

What a joy it will be to someday use your freedom to help others out of the same pit!

That's the beauty of God's healing. Beauty for ashes. He'll take your weakness and turn it into strength.

Please let me pray with you.

> Heavenly Father,
>
> I have been through hurt, betrayal, pain, shame, and so many other things that have separated me from You. Right now I join with the heart of Christ to heal those scars and wounds through the power of Your Holy Spirit. I pray peace that passes all understanding to wrap around those spiritual abscesses, drawing out the poison and soothing the pain.
>
> Father, You are the only GOOD addiction. I pray I would get a taste of Your sweet presence right now. May I truly sense Your love drawing me close and filling every gaping need. I join with Your declaration that You have hope and a future—good things—for me. May the joy of Christ's resurrection overflow every facet of my being. May Your holy angels beat back the forces of darkness. Thank you, Heavenly Father, for turning my weakness into strength that will in turn set many others free.
>
> Hallelujah, Father, for making beauty from ashes.
>
> Through Jesus' Holy Name, Amen.

An effective organization that may even have a meeting near you is Celebrate Recovery. Celebrate Recovery addresses hurts, habits, and hang-ups with spiritual support, group therapy and twelve-step programs: CelebrateRecovery.com

CHAPTER 23

I SCREWED UP. NOW WHAT?

"The most important step a man can take is the one
he takes right after he's blown it."
WINKIE PRATNEY

Dilyse was so eager for love, she jumped headlong into marriage before coming to terms with the fact that her mate was abusive and controlling. She eventually got out of the marriage but the scars remained for her and her children. Through her prayers and attempts to understand what drew her to marry this type of man, Dilyse decided to go back to school. Over the years, even as she had to deal with troubled teens and an angry ex, she got her degree as a licensed Christian Family Therapist.

Hundreds of families and individuals have walked the long road to healing with Dilyse, safe in the knowledge she too continues to walk that road. Dilyse says she believes this is the best way to bring joy from the pain she has endured. "Every time I see someone draw close to God and begin to make healthy relational decisions, I can thank God for my pain because it gave me a way to ease theirs. Somehow, that makes it all worthwhile."

When I was in college I knew a young couple, Donna and Dave. Both had been raised without a moral code regarding sex. It was just something that went along with an affectionate relationship. However, when they became fully convinced God wanted sex to be reserved for marriage, *they stopped.* There was no moaning and groaning or anger and they didn't grovel in the guilt of their past. With childlike trust, they simply stopped and turned around and God met them with open arms. In turn, their relationship with God and each other was marked by the choice to put Him first.

But what if you did something wrong and you knew beyond a shadow of a doubt that you were blowing it, but you did it anyway? Do you still deserve forgiveness? Shouldn't you suffer a bit more?

WHAT MAKES THE DIFFERENCE?

From Genesis on down, God kept reaching out to His people, trying over and over, generation after generation, to keep them from stuff that would destroy them. There were instructions about sex, instructions about what to eat, instructions about money, instructions about planting and harvesting, sickness, social justice, etc. etc.

But, if you miss the stories of redemption among all the rules, you're missing a major chunk of God's personality.

Over and over God's people blew it. Adam and Eve did the *one thing* they were told not to do. Their son, Cain, murdered his brother Abel. Abraham and Sarah lost faith in God's promise for making them parents and decided to have a baby through Sarah's maidservant. Jacob tricked

Esau out of his birthright and Esau was so angry about it he would have killed Jacob if Jacob hadn't run away. King Saul feared people more than he feared God. David committed adultery with Bathsheba and, to cover the sin, had her husband killed. Solomon married tons of foreign wives who brought their idol worship with them to Israel. Peter denied he knew Jesus three times to save his own skin. Paul persecuted, imprisoned, and even had followers of Christ killed. Even spiritual superhero Moses had a bit of a temper tantrum and hit a rock when God told him to speak to it to provide water for the thirsty Israelites. But that was nothing compared to his younger days when he murdered an Egyptian.

Rather a motley crew, eh? And this is just a small sample of Bible all-stars. All made mistakes ranging from minor infractions to sexual immorality and even murder. Some remained separated from God, yet others emerged closer to Him than ever. What made the difference?

REPENTANCE AND REDEMPTION

Repentance means turning away from sin and walking in the opposite direction. *Redemption* is restoration—returning to a place of "wholeness." Wholeness or *Holiness* can only come from God.

Think of it like a ransom paid to buy you out of slavery. When we choose to go against God's commandments, we choose to be slaves to sin. Call it slavery to selfishness, slavery to evil, but whatever you call it, the fact remains, you are mastered by what you obey.

It could be something as seemingly harmless as sugar or as overtly destructive as drugs, pornography, murderous rage, sexual exploits, or rampant greed but *whatever controls you, that's your god.*

Bottom line definition of sin: sin separates us from God.

HISTORIC WATER HOLE ENCOUNTER

In the fourth chapter of John we are told about the time when Jesus meets a fallen woman. This lady is an outcast on so many levels, she's even despised among her own people, the Samaritans, people the Jews viewed as unclean because they had mixed their Jewish blood and Jewish faith with foreign blood and faith. It's as if Jesus had a homing device that drew him to the lowest of the low, the person who was most rejected, most riddled with self-hatred, and felt least worthy of God.

For a bit of background on this woman, we need to understand the society of Jesus' day. Men could divorce or "put away" their wives, but the reverse was not possible. This woman had been "put away" five times, and the man she was living with hadn't even bothered to marry her. Perhaps she couldn't have children, which was one of the major reasons men divorced women. If this was the case, people thought a woman's womb was cursed and would assume God had his reasons for punishing her. She is obviously even avoiding the other women in her town since she is coming to the well at noon, during the heat of the day, whereas the customary time was in the morning or evening when it was cool.

Can you imagine the way this woman must have walked? How she must have kept her eyes to the ground as she approached Jesus? Here she is, rejected on all levels—by reason of religion, sex, childlessness (writer's speculation), and gender—but she is the one Jesus arranges to meet.

Jesus broke several taboos by even speaking to her since the Jews treated sin as something contagious, like a disease, therefore their way to remain holy was to avoid contact with sinners. But Jesus didn't stop there. He asked her to give him a drink from the well. What? A Jew would share the water of half-breeds?

One gets the impression the woman is so astounded by Jesus' odd behavior that she is shocked into honest communication. "You, a Jew, would ask me, a Samaritan *woman,* for a drink?"

Then Jesus intrigues her even more. "If you realized Who was talking to you, you would be asking me for a drink, and I could give you water that would make you never thirst again."

Water she won't have to lug home every day? Awesome!

The conversation becomes a bit of a theological debate as the woman points out how the Jews say the Samaritan place of worship is bogus. Jesus shoots that one down by telling her the building is not what counts because soon people will be able to "worship in Spirit and in truth." In other words, it's a matter of heart that makes people right with God, not a geological location. Okay, two areas of rejection down, but Jesus is just getting started.

"Go get your husband," he tells her.

I can practically see her downcast eyes and hunched shoulders as she answers, "I have no husband."

But I can also imagine Jesus leaning down a bit to look in her eyes. "That's right. You've had five husbands, and the man you're living with is not your husband."

Ooh! Busted. But Jesus keeps on talking to her. She gets it that Jesus must be some kind of prophet, after all, He just read her mail, but Jesus wants her to get the real point, that He *is* the living water she needs. She sets up the next interchange by bringing up the Messiah Who, when He comes, will answer all their questions.

Jesus spells it out, leaving no room for misunderstanding, *"I, the One speaking to you, Am He."*

She didn't even know his name, but she immediately believed Him. She had never known a person who would know her *and* love her. This man *must* be from God! Jesus' unconditional love and power were irresistible and undeniable.

What did the woman do? She ran to get anyone who would listen. "Come and meet this man who told me everything I have done. Could this be the Messiah?"

This woman, rejected by society and even by religion, becomes the mouthpiece for salvation for her entire town!

BEAUTY FOR ASHES

In a song called *Grace* by U2, Bono sings:

> *"Grace... what left a mark, no longer stings*
> *Because grace makes beauty out of ugly things."*

When God gets hold of those areas of your life that have been destroying you, He will turn those weaknesses into strength. Just like the Samaritan woman at the well who, *because of* the hopelessness and rejection in her life, was the perfect conduit of Jesus' unconditional love, so too your circumstances and screw-ups can become beauty in God's hands.

Interpretation: No matter what you've done, God is big enough to deal with it and even make it your greatest strength.

> In my early twenties, I took a trip to Germany. It was summertime so the windows were open at night. One morning I woke to an awful stench in the air. I was raised on a ranch so I knew what it was—cow poop. The lady of the house informed me it was fertilizing time. The surrounding fields had been coated with a thick layer of fresh, horribly

fragrant cow manure. Talk about your potpourri! But there was no denying, those Germans kept some beautifully green and productive fields.

No matter what you've been through, it's not too late. Even if you have a lifetime of regret, shit makes great fertilizer. (Sorry Mom) God can take our impossibilities and transform them into miracles. Consequences are no fun, but in God's hands, even the worst can be turned into a fresh start for you and others who can learn from your mistakes.

It's called beauty for ashes. That's God's specialty.

RACHEAL

Racheal was raised in a loving, church-going home, but there came a time, although she had been taught sex was "wrong" until marriage, that she chose sexual immorality. "I wish I had learned that sex is meant to be a good/wonderful thing because God created it," says Racheal. "I wish I had been taught that it is the most precious gift you can save and give in its entirety to the one you marry. It's not that my parents taught me the opposite; it's just that it hadn't been explained to me that way."

Racheal had a boyfriend in high school and plenty of unsupervised time to experiment. "I wasn't having intercourse, just everything else, so I thought I wasn't having sex. I've since discovered that those experiences took a piece of me."

Eventually, Racheal decided in college to become sexually active. "I came home, had sex with the 'right' guy to get it done, and then felt like that made it okay to be with the other person. I justified that I had given myself to the right guy whom I would end up marrying; but for now, I wanted to have a good time. This decision ended up leading me into an unwanted pregnancy."

Among Racheal's college friends, sex, pregnancy, and abortions were the norm.

Therefore Racheal, ignoring those who tried to dissuade her, chose to have an abortion. For a while, that decision just empowered her to continue with her life of casual sex. But eventually, the hidden shame worked its way to the surface and she prayed that God would forgive her.

Years later, she attended a post-abortion group meeting. More shame and regret bubbled to the surface. But through the pain, Racheal found a new passion to counsel women struggling with an unwanted pregnancy.

"Abortion," says Racheal, "is only a quick fix for others involved in that woman's life. The fear of pregnancy is temporary, but the consequences of abortion remain for a lifetime."

Racheal still regrets the decisions she made as a young woman but she is grateful for the chance to prevent others from making the same mistakes. Her pain, in God's hands, has become a driving passion—

1. To help women understand that abortion is no easy fix

2. To fight for the lives of babies who cannot speak for themselves

3. To help women through post-abortion emotional pain

The pain of Racheal's past spurs her on to help other young ladies in similar circumstances. Her life is an amazing picture of God's grace.

SPIRITUAL HEALING

Do you really think you're hiding anything from God? Do you really think your sin is so special that, of all the sinners throughout history, you have maxed out the grace that drew Jesus to the cross?

You are not beyond the reach of God's love. It is higher and wider and deeper than our puny brains could ever imagine.

Here's your assignment. Take your greatest pain—that thing that goads you at the darnedest times and might be something you think God could never forgive—and plunk it down before Him. See what happens.

Cast that pain/regret /unforgiveness /stupid choice/addiction/hatred/ fear, etc. down. Ask God to forgive you and help you forgive others— especially yourself. Paint a picture in your mind of that horrible weight you've been carrying (only you are intimately acquainted enough with your personal monster to do this) and ask God to cut the chains that thing has wrapped around you. State the fact that Jesus is bigger than that weight even if your emotions can't fully believe it.

Remember, whatever controls your thoughts, words, and emotions—that is your god. Shove it off the throne and just see what God can do. It's a start. It's setting your foot on a new path.

NEITHER DO I CONDEMN YOU

One day, the religious leaders threw a woman at Jesus' feet and told him she had been "caught in the act of adultery." (John 8: 1-11) The law said such a woman should be taken outside the city and stoned to death. These leaders were attempting to catch Jesus between law and love, but He was too smart for them. Jesus knelt down and began to write in the dirt. Some believe He was writing the names of the accusers' girlfriends. We don't know for sure what He wrote, but all He said was one simple sentence. "Let he who is without sin cast the first stone." One by one the accusers dropped their stones and walked away. Jesus asked her, "Where are your accusers?"

"They are gone," the woman answered.

"Neither do I condemn you," Jesus said. "Go and sin no more."

Later, a known prostitute (the scriptures do not identify her by name in Luke's gospel so it is unclear if she is the same woman) entered a home where Jesus was having dinner, knelt at his feet, and began to weep so much that she washed His feet with her tears. As the people looked on in horror at this public display of intimacy, she began to dry Jesus' feet with her hair. Once they were clean, she anointed his feet with expensive perfume. The woman's overwhelming love and gratitude drove her to lavish lengths and, since her reputation had been in tatters, she had nothing to lose. She fully realized her need of Jesus. She had lived as an outcast so long, God's passionate love and acceptance touched her in a profound way, in a way the religious leaders, who thought their obedience to rules made them worthy, *could not begin to understand.*

Jesus made this woman feel more loved and clean than a virgin bride. Her depth of devotion to Him matched the depth of healing. ***His love removed her shame.*** (Luke 7:36-50)

No matter what you've done, Jesus longs to embrace you just as you are. He won't see you as damaged goods when you give Him your sin. What He offers is a fresh start with a clean slate. It might not erase all the negative consequences of bad choices, but you won't walk through them alone because God will be with you, providing grace and courage every step of the way.

When we left Victoria Jackson, she was a divorced, famous, single mom with an unpredictable comedy career and a backlog of regret. Soon, however, Victoria experienced firsthand God's overwhelming love, redemption, and mercy.

Her last year at Saturday Night Live, Victoria's high school sweetheart, Paul, came back into her life. His marriage, too, had ended and they were both surprised to find they had another chance at love. They agreed that this time they would do things God's way.

Victoria has the rare perspective of experiencing both; sex devoid of joy *and* sex as God intended. She describes lovemaking with her first husband as, "He was just bored, like a blow-up doll, because he had had sex with *everybody*. I was just another notch on his bedpost."

But her honeymoon with Paul was exactly the opposite. "I told Paul once that I almost wished we had had sex when we were teenagers because I was so much younger and prettier and skinnier then and he said, 'Oh no! I'm so glad we didn't because when we did (on their wedding night), it was beautiful and right.'"

Victoria says, "We actually fell off the bed laughing and crying at the same time. It was deep and meaningful, mentally, physically, and spiritually."

Always the comedienne, Victoria emphasizes her feelings about sex God's way with a joke delivered in her childlike voice. "There's a new Playboy for married men. It has the same centerfold every month."

Victoria explains. "That's how the world sees it, but the reality is you can't dissect it, and you can't explain it because (married) sex is a mystery and there's nothing snickery about it. There's so much more involved. It's mysterious. It's never boring, never the same, and *always* like the first time."

Looking back at her past, Victoria has this insight. "Following God's way is best, but He forgives and redeems and He can make beauty from ashes. It seems that the more people are forgiven the more grateful they are for forgiveness. I can understand and help others because I've been there."

In this chapter, we've explored so many stories of *God's forgiveness,* the freedom of *repentance,* and the joy of *redemption.* What story of redemption does God want to tell with your life?

For an incredibly powerful example of God's redemption and restoration, watch Lisa Luby-Ryan's I Am Second video.

CHAPTER 24

WHAT IF YOU HAD NO CHOICE?

Unfortunately, many don't have the advantage of a protective, loving family and may even have choice stripped away while they're still children. In this age of early indoctrination to sexuality, children need to be lovingly forewarned and forearmed in an age-appropriate way as soon as possible.

MICHELLE

Michelle and Adam have one of the sweetest marriages I've ever witnessed. They adore one another and their five children are growing up in a wonderfully positive environment where Mom and Dad's love for each other is the central glue for an awesome family dynamic. But, when one hears about Michelle's childhood and troubled teen years, it's obvious God's grace is mind-boggling and He *loves* to heal and redeem His kids.

You see, when Michelle was only seven years old, two older cousins began to abuse her sexually. "I never told anybody," says Michelle, "because I was convinced I was a 'dirty girl' and it was somehow my fault."

Later, Michelle endured other instances of abuse but, with a child's ability to avoid reality, those memories became fuzzy for her until she was sixteen and they began to push to the surface. "I began having nightmares where I was above myself, seeing the abuse," she says.

At the same time, Michelle's boyfriend, her best friend, cheated on her. She was devastated and, in the midst of this painful breakup, another trusted friend, a girl, began to make sexual advances. "I said to myself, 'It must be that guys hurt me. Well, *she* would never hurt me.' So that relationship began and went on a few months until my parents found out and confronted me about it."

In the midst of the confrontation about Michelle's girlfriend, she told her parents about the abuse by her cousins. Her parents were shocked and heartbroken.

With her world seemingly falling apart, Michelle ran away from home. "It's amazing that I survived that time," says Michelle. "I went through so many scary things—drugs, relationships, had to drop out of school—but I can see now how God really rescued me."

Eventually, her half-sister's family took her in but they insisted Michelle get a job to help with expenses. When she stopped by her parents' house to retrieve her birth certificate for a job interview, her four-year-old little sister begged her to "change her clothes and come home," since she had overheard Michelle's father say Michelle needed to "make some changes" if she was to move back.

Back at her half-sister's house, Michelle felt God speaking to her, telling her that, if she would go home, He would be with her and things would be alright. Michelle just thought she had taken too many pills. "But God was like a thick blanket, saying, 'Go home, I'm gonna make it okay. I don't care what you've done. I love you,'" Michelle recalls.

"I knelt down and asked God to forgive me. I called my girlfriend and told her I was making lots of changes, called my parents and told them I was ready. They put me in a private school, and I got caught up in my studies." At that point, Michelle says she had to break ties with all her old friends because, "they were all bad for me."

That was the summer when she met her future husband, Adam. "He was in a band called *Winnowing Poets* and they asked me to sing with them. We practiced all the time and soon Adam was my best friend and, soon after that, it was more than friendship. He knew everything about me and still loved me."

She and Adam were married when Michelle was only eighteen. One thing Michelle says she never had to deal with was confusing the abuse she had suffered as a child with the healthy sexual relations she enjoys with her husband. "Immediately when we got married I really felt safe just being completely his and he was completely mine. I never had a struggle comparing Adam with the abuse because there's no comparison between love and that."

Even with marriage to a wonderful man, however, Michelle admits there are struggles. "As I watch the course of my life, it's like the Lord continues to want healing. All the stuff I thought I'd really been freed from when I was a teenager will come up and I will feel like the broken little girl again and God will say, 'Let's mend this.'"[15]

SARAH J.R. SMITH "PRECARIOUS YATES"

Since Sarah is an excellent author, I asked her to tell her story in her own words.

"When I was 11, someone I trusted completely violated my trust in the worst way. It wasn't just once. It was multiple times over the course of six months. I hurt in ways I didn't even think were possible. I had just experienced my parents' public and very brutal custody battle over us children, so I knew pain. This was worse than anything I'd ever known. I was so traumatized that I started experiencing seizures and blacked out memories of anything having happened.

But no matter how hard I tried, I couldn't black out the pain. There was a constant ache, and after each seizure that constant ache grew.

When I obsessed over a cute boy, I would apply that ache to a longing for an intimate relationship. Over and over I ached for that intimate relationship until boys started noticing me back.

From the age of 13 to 20, I had sex with so many boyfriends and girlfriends that I actually lost count. Each time I started a relationship, I was so sure that this experience would be better than the last time.

Every time the pain in my heart increased and I grew more and more numb. Dating was pleasant for a moment, but it caused more harm than good.

---

15   To learn more about Adam and Michelle Palmer's story and music visit: AdamPalmerAuthor.com & twitter.com/michellepalmer

I was 20 when Jesus found me. I was broken. I was so sure that I was beyond repair. It's remarkable how complete His healing was. Not only did He deal with the pain and the shame that threatened to smother me, He brought a godly man into my life who loved me in spite of my past."[16]

The Need for Healing

If our earliest experiences of sex are riddled with guilt, shame, fear, and betrayal, those are the feelings that will bubble to the surface, polluting what God would like to give. These memories may be buried as they were for my friend Susan who did not recall the sexual abuse at the hands of her grandfather until she was in her forties. "A child has no context, no words, for what they can't understand so they tend to block it out."

A victim of rape or child molestation bears the weight of another's sin forced on their body. But—God is still a God of miracles, waiting to take even the most horrendous circumstances and transform them into beauty and strength—the very thing to reach a hurting, dying world.

---

16   To learn more about Sarah J.R. Smith who writes under the pen name Precarious Yates, go to precariousyates.com

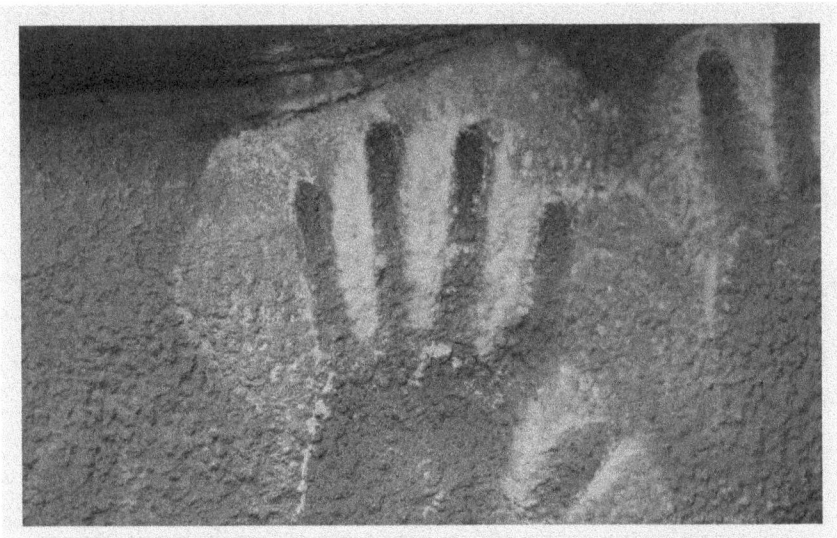

The Stuff of Nightmares

I don't share this next portion to gross you out, shock you or to stretch your imagination of the horrors evil people can perpetrate upon the innocent and powerless—namely children. I share this because, if we are going to approach the subject of childhood sexual trauma and abuse, we must also stretch our faith that a Good God is willing and able to redeem and even make strength from weakness, just like the Bible says.[17]

We know a remarkable physical therapist who is a noted, gifted, and extremely effective expert at dealing with pelvic pain. Due to her specialty, over the course of her near-30 years of practice, she has encountered approximately 50 patients who are victims of extreme, ritualistic, sexual abuse. We're talking the horrific abuse one finds in

---

17   And He said to me, "My grace is sufficient for you, for My strength is made perfect in weakness." Therefore most gladly I will rather boast in my infirmities, that the power of Christ may rest upon me. 2 Cor 12:9

horror movies, the kind we would like to believe is only a product of overactive imaginations.

Alas, it is not.

The therapist says, "Generally, if these abuse victims survive to adulthood, it is a miracle, since they suffer so horribly and feel so alone. Most people will not believe their stories or they may have shoved these experiences so deeply into their psyches that they are forgotten." However, due to the nature of her work, dealing with trauma and rehabilitation to female organs and intense pelvic pain, the traumatic memories are triggered.

"The first time this happened, I had been in practice only about a year," she says. Suddenly the patient, a young woman in her early twenties, started speaking to her in another voice, the voice of a demon. Fortunately, the patient's father was waiting for her out in the lobby so the therapist brought him in to be a witness to this occurrence. Upon further investigation, the father learned of horrible abuse that had happened to the young woman when she was a child—perpetrated by her grandmother.

Often, the patients who have endured abuse beyond our worst nightmares, develop what is known as Multiple Personality Disorder, (also referred to as Dissociative Identity Disorder[18]) in order to deal with the trauma. "For this reason," the therapist says, "cults and covens

---

18   The Mayo Clinic description of Dissociative Disorders: Dissociative disorders usually develop as a way to cope with trauma. The disorders most often form in children subjected to long-term physical, sexual or emotional abuse or, less often, a home environment that's frightening or highly unpredictable. The stress of war or natural disasters also can bring on dissociative disorders.

that practice this abuse look for extremely intelligent children who can survive the abuse by dissociative reaction, splitting into separate personalities, that act as a sort of family that gather around the core of the child like protective buffers." This phenomenon, of course, is completely different than the effect of demonic presence since that voice is only the deepest, inconceivable hate.

"It's actually quite remarkable the intelligence this sort of complicated protective system requires," the therapist notes. But due to her work at addressing deep pain that was caused by the overwhelming trauma they have endured, often these 'inner children' will speak to her during a therapy session. Unfortunately, the therapist has found that many classically trained psychiatrists and psychologists are not prepared to deal with these occurrences on a spiritual level and will tell the inner children to "go away."

"But these inner children," she says, "have a story to tell that they desperately need to get off their chest and they are seeking someone to trust." These individuals have so often hidden from society, and been unable to maintain what we would consider normal relationships because they endure not only the torment of horrific memories but also the constant harassment from evil forces that have been assigned to them or even "married to them" during perverted ritual sacraments. Thus they suffer horribly in isolation. And if they have endured psychiatrists and psychologists who dismiss the existence of spiritual phenomena or exhibit impatience and/or disbelief toward the inner children, these victims also suffer the added trauma of not being believed.

We must understand that when we profess Christ as our Savior and Lord, we are to grow more and more into His likeness so we too, as the therapist has modeled, can provide a place of help and healing to the most abused and marginalized in our world. The extremes Christ went to when He chose to die to pay for ALL that separates us from our Holy

Heavenly Father, is more than sufficient to lead these tortured souls out of their prisons of fear and constant torment. The missing link is the Body of Christ, we who are called by His name, who can tend to sleep in the light while many suffer in a living hell. The therapist and the very few who understand this horrible travesty are not supposed to stand alone beside these victims. Scripture says God "sets the lonely in families." These atrocities have been committed by a group of scarred and depraved individuals who many times were the victims of abuse when they were young. How can this cycle end?

> *"When My people who are called by my name will humble themselves and pray and seek my face and turn from their wicked ways, then will I hear from Heaven, I will forgive their sin and will heal their land." II Chron. 7:14*

Satan may be the master perverter of sex and family and every good, perfect gift that God has given, but God is the great Redeemer.

Bottom line, we—you and I—need to seek and live in God's full freedom from shame, perversion and fear so when we encounter God's children in need of healing, our faith will go deep into His power and authority to end their suffering.

Holy Father,

You see our worst; our fears, our unforgiveness, our moments of torment and lapses in faith. Though we are imperfect, we ask to be channels of your perfect love to Your suffering children. You love to make beauty from ashes and you delight in turning our greatest weakness into strength to help others.

May we stand with You against every work of darkness and truly bring Your light for those who are blinded with pain. We choose to forgive those who have harmed and even abused us. We will not allow them to live rent-free in our minds any longer. We cut those ties to those who have hurt us and choose to bond completely with your goodness and love and mind-blowing grace. May we abide in you daily so we can become more like You, know you better, and be Your hands and feet and arms of love to those who are desperate for healing.

In Jesus' holy name,

Amen

CHAPTER 25

STAY ALERT!

Please listen to some wisdom from the trenches. Don't get too comfortable. Remember, you're in a battle. Ya gotta be ready to duck—or run—at any moment.

With my college boyfriend, while the training and prayer were lifelines in the midst of marathon kissing sessions, what was my Achilles Heel?

Smug Pride.

"I'm not like that."
"I can stop any time."
"We can handle it."

I told myself these and other naïve lies as if I was different from every red-blooded young adult from the dawn of time.

Sex is a powerful thing. Don't let anyone tell you otherwise—not even yourself. If you think it's something you can toy with, experiment with, and "handle" think again. You are NOT the one exception to the rule. If you give yourself enough sexual rope you WILL hang yourself. Remember:

IF YOU FAIL TO PLAN, YOU PLAN TO FAIL!

I was nineteen when stupidity almost won the day.

I was babysitting a little boy for the weekend and my boyfriend came over. The mom said my boyfriend was welcome so that made it okay, right? We got the little boy to bed, kissed a while, then I went upstairs to bed and left my boyfriend watching TV on the couch where he was going to sleep. A couple hours later, after coming across an erotic movie while channel surfing, he decided to come upstairs to continue our make-out session.

I was more than a little vulnerable and, when I did have a coherent thought, it was mostly of kicking aside the covers and going for it. In that moment, even when my personal preferences didn't agree, the vow of waiting until marriage bubbled up in panic and my heart's cry was, *"Please God. No!"*

I said those words out loud and soon the boyfriend exited stage left.

Okay class. Shall we go over a few of the stupid choices that led to this situation?

1. He was over when I was "on the job." DUMB.
2. I didn't kick him out the door when it got late. DUMBER.
3. I overestimated our sexual backbone (pride).
4. I shoulda locked the friggin' door!

Suffice it to say, I was so glad I didn't get what my pride and stupidity deserved that night. Even in the middle of major temptation, God answered when I cried out to Him.

Again, what was the vital missing ingredient in my calculations? **Humility**. My pride in believing that once we had agreed NOT to have sex *we were safe*, set me up for a fall.

I don't claim to have all the answers. I don't know why I came through that night with virginity intact when others in similar situations have a different ending to their story. But I'm grateful and I'm convinced ninety-nine percent of the credit is due to God's grace (and probably wiser Christians in my life who were faithful to pray for me) even when I walked smugly into a foolish trap. I'm grateful my boyfriend had a conscience even though it didn't kick in soon enough for him to change the channel. I'm *very* grateful he was unselfish enough to honor my wishes when I said the word "no." I'm grateful for the gift of panic that bubbled past physical desire and made me call out for God's help.

I'm also grateful for the long talk my boyfriend and I had the next day where he admitted to the erotic show that had worked him into his extremely turned-on state. It was one of several red flags that signaled the end of our relationship. Besides, I was nowhere near ready to be married to him or anyone else, so why would I remain in a dating relationship that was pushing toward sex?

Even without the act of sex, the disentangling process after a year and a half of exclusive dating was painful. In retrospect, I wish we hadn't allowed as much physical passion in our relationship as we did because the un-bonding hurt—a lot. Even though he wasn't my mate for life, he was still a dear friend with many wonderful qualities who didn't deserve to be strung along. How I wish I had been confident enough to pull out of the relationship sooner. But I was selfish, insecure, and enjoyed the fact I finally had a boyfriend like "normal" girls. I had dates on the weekends and someone who made me feel special, wanted, and womanly. Yes, I was using him to love myself.

So, what plan would have prevented the almost-disastrous babysitting debacle?

No sleepovers—especially unchaperoned ones. All it takes is opportunity, fatigue, and the belief your standards are bulletproof and BAM! Those standards are blown to hell.

CHAPTER 26

ON SHACKIN' UP

If you are aiming for a healthy love that will last a lifetime, be careful. Shortcuts to bliss are available, but will only lead to roadblocks and/or sabotage.

One of the most insidious deceptions today is the mirage of marriage offered by living together before matrimony. What are the logical sounding persuasions to make it attractive?

1. You get a more realistic view of life with this person.
2. Sharing expenses makes sense.
3. Less time and money spent on dates equals less waste
4. You can make sure the two of you are sexually compatible

Wow. Those all sound pretty good. What's the big deal?

Let's take a gander at what's around the bend of this tempting shortcut.

Reason #1—A More "Realistic" view

I loved playing house as a kid. In my pretending, the dolls never talked back, the food was plastic so there was always plenty, everyone always got along and—the real beauty—if I got bored, I could quit and play something else.

Ever been part of a live production, play, or musical performance? Right before opening night, the cast and crew will have a dress rehearsal where they run through the show from start to finish with make-up, costumes, lights, and all the other factors that will have to mesh during the "real" show. I've taken part in several productions and, while dress rehearsals are a vital way to make sure we've "thought of everything," I've *never* seen a dress rehearsal where people treated it like the real thing. The director calls "Cut," someone forgets a line and drops out of character, someone trips and everyone breaks up with laughter, a piece of scenery falls and everyone stops cold to fix it. But that's okay. It's not the real thing. There's no investment in "The Show Must Go On" because it's not "The Show," we're just pretending. If things get to be a mess, we can abandon this run-through and start another.

Opening Night, however, is a completely different animal. The energy backstage is electric. *This* is what everything has been for—*this* audience and *this* moment. The players are hyper-focused. *Nothing*, at that moment matters but *that moment*. Everyone is fully invested and there's no turning back. No matter what happens, this is the real show and it *will go on*. A million dress rehearsals could never equal the adrenalin rush of opening night.

Perhaps sports are your venue. Could practice against another team where no championship is at stake ever compare to the intensity of that first whistle in the Super Bowl with millions cheering and everything—career, self-worth, finances, even your body—on the line?

That babysitting experience with my boyfriend *felt* like what I imagined marriage would be. At least I thought it did at the time. We made dinner together, even had a cute little kid to read to and tuck in bed, we sat up chatting and watching TV just like couples do, and I even went up to bed as he stayed downstairs to unwind a bit more.

Only problem was, it was just pretend. We had skipped all sorts of building blocks in our relational architecture. Investment was non-existent. There had been no public commitment. There was no blessing from our families. The child wasn't ours. We hadn't bought the food. We hadn't paid for the beautiful home. All the trappings were someone else's investment. And at the time, we had no clue what those trappings truly cost in the way of selflessness and commitment. It came easily and we were taking it for granted, because the *mirage* of marriage felt real and was very seductive. It had all the warm fuzzies of permanent commitment with none of the investment.

Choosing to forego marriage and skip straight to shared lodging is a bit like that. You get to enjoy the benefits of sharing a home minus the tedious stuff like including their family in this momentous decision and pledging your life to love, honor, cherish, and stick with this person no matter what.

But when you build a house and ignore the foundation, it's easy for something, or someone, to blow your house in.

Even if you truly feel you can cohabitate without having sex, what message are you sending to the rest of the world? Whether you like it or not, God makes it clear that followers of Christ are to keep their lives above reproach so no one will be influenced due to a lifestyle of compromise. And what about those who may follow your lead who don't possess your superhuman self-control? God makes it clear in three of the gospels (Matt. 18, Mark 9, and Luke 17) that anyone who causes one of His children to stumble would be better off to "have a large millstone hung around their neck and to be drowned in the depths of the sea." Jesus wasn't messin' around.

Besides, take it from someone who still benefits from choosing God's order of marriage *before* cohabitation. (Yeah, I know I squeezed by only with the grace of God) The real thing is too special to miss. When Mark and I drove away from our wedding toward our highly anticipated honeymoon with no ghosts of lovers past tagging along for the ride, it was no cheap substitute. No regrets. No shame. No fear. Just exclusive intimacy that sealed our covenant for life. It's a spark that re-sparks and has kept on igniting.

That first sexual, spiritual, mental, emotional experience was pure magic. Sex was equated with fun, joy, and the excitement of pent up sexual release in an atmosphere of "Wow! This is *okay* now!" On occasion we still marvel at the fact that God is as pleased with our intimacy as he is with our prayers. The overwhelming gratitude we felt the first night of our honeymoon still reigns supreme.

Reason #2—Sharing Expenses Makes More Sense

When I was dating Mark and things were tight financially, I would feel guilty if he offered me money. After all, it was "his" and my problems were "mine." It was amazing how that attitude flipped after our wedding. It was no longer "yours and mine" it was "ours." We were a team. We were *all in*. We had trekked through commitment, family issues, money discussions, baby talks, saving sex talks, and even the overwhelming pressure cooker of wedding details. Along the way, with every wedding invitation, we could have backed out. But every issue and struggle also revealed more reasons to love this man who took my hand and asked God's advice. We weren't playing house. The full price was paid. This was the real thing; adrenalin rush, cheering audience, and all.

Playing house is nothing like the real thing. The real thing is much more… REAL. Building a home together, with full responsibility and commitment, is both harder and more glorious. Sure, commitment involves sacrifice and responsibility, but it also includes deep peace and the legal and spiritual benefits that cut fear. Something supernatural occurs when the repeating of vows comes before physical consummation. When our bodies came together for the first time, that first sex carried more gravity. It was like signing our names in blood on each other's heart.

Intense emotional responses in our bodies etch themselves on our spirits. If that first experience of "playing house" involves no commitment, lack of investment, and the "yours and mine" attitude, those emotions will be present like an old lover when you step into marriage. That sense of a "real" opening night, of that first snap of the ball at the Super Bowl, of that exchange of rings and sex that signs in blood, cannot be recreated when you have cheated the process before and played house. In that case, the "dress rehearsal" works in reverse. Shacking up doesn't just uncover possible glitches in a relationship, it creates them. It sabotages intimacy because the two of you have practiced keeping one foot out the back door "just in case." You get your cake and eat it too, only to find the cake is kinda tasteless because it's not the cake according to God's recipe.

Oswald Chambers, author of the devotional classic *My Utmost for His Highest*, wrote:

> "Temptation is a suggested short cut to the realization of the highest at which I aim – not towards what I understand as evil, but towards what I understand as good." [19]

In God's recipe for a healthy, vibrant marriage, living together before marriage is a shortcut that injects poison. Sure there are examples of couples who seem to be okay even though they chose living together before matrimony, but in architectural terms, you are building a huge tower without getting the foundation right. That's a set-up for cave-in and collapse.

---

19   *My Utmost For His Highest* By Oswald Chambers (Buy this in hard cover. It's a classic to be read again and again.)

In Isaiah 55, God says, *"As the heavens are higher than the earth, so are My ways higher than your ways and my thoughts than your thoughts."*

Also, Proverbs 3:5-6 says, *"Trust in the Lord with all of your heart and lean not on your own understanding. Acknowledge the Lord* (consider God's desire first) *in all of your ways and He will make your paths straight."*

Reason #3—Ensure "Sexual Compatability"

Once, a young woman asked Mark and I how we, "made sure we were sexually compatible" since we didn't have sex until after we were married. Here we were, married twenty-plus years, and we both looked at each other, mouths a bit agape, and laughed. Then we asked her a question. "What does 'sexually compatible' even mean? All we know is we have tons of fun, it's ours alone, and no one needs to tell us we're 'compatible' because it's all about pleasing the person we love the most."

Consider this. Perhaps we are so "compatible" precisely because we waited.

We never experienced sex outside God's laws, so we have felt only joy in the midst of it. If I had felt separated from God with that first sexual high with Mark, that feeling would have tainted the experience and, again, would have tattooed sex with an element of guilt rather than unfettered joy.

> If you love somebody and you've given it enough time, and you know they're "the one," then you're going to be compatible. Living together is an excuse to not get married, to try to make things easier on yourself."
>
> WONDER-HUBBY MARK

Throughout this book, I have emphasized the spiritual and emotional elements that accompany the physical aspects of sex. Whether you like it or not, you are hardwired to enjoy the experience of sex more if there is no guilt or fear attached to the act.

Therefore, the very people who encourage you to "ensure sexual compatibility" are unwitting saboteurs.

> "But if I keep saying 'No!' to sex, won't that scar my sexual expression later?"

I can laugh at that question now, but I admit the thought occurred to me, the twenty-six-year-old virgin, before I married.

Was it hard for Mark and I to turn that corner when all the "waits" became "Go for it?" God even had a hand in that little detail.

About a week before our wedding, I woke from a fairly explicit dream involving Mark and thought, "Ohmigosh! I'd better apologize to God and get that out of my head!"

Know what? The deep impression as I prayed was of God's huge smile, like He was saying, "That dream was from Me. I'm just helping to readjust your thinking."

Wow! God was preparing me, after twenty-six years, to enjoy sex. What an amazing God. The One Who helped me save sex for marriage was helping to make the transition smooth.

God is good.

Get that through your head. His aim is not to steal your fun but to keep you from heartbreak and regret so that, when you give yourself body, mind, and spirit to your mate, it's a lasting, healthy, lifelong bond.

PATRICIA & BRANDON

Patricia and Brandon met in high school and professed their love three months later. These high school sweethearts stayed together through college and decided in their mid-twenties it was time to move in together. They planned to be married someday, but this seemed to be a logical step into adulthood and financial independence. A couple years into their cohabitation, they both got closer to God and were baptized. Finally, Patricia stated, "We're going to have to do this right." So, Patricia and Brandon decided they would choose to be abstinent until they got married. They made the tough choice to move back in with their parents to get on a sound financial footing and, as Patricia says, to please God with their relationship. "We gave ourselves a goal to be back on our feet in a year, meaning financially stable."

Both say it was difficult to make the adjustment back to living with their parents. "It definitely was hard struggling with feeling I was not progressing as an adult," says Patricia.

In the coming months, as Brandon and Patricia tried to do things right, other issues of their relationship pushed forward. "It didn't matter that we had been together for 12 years. We still had to start at square one because now we were looking through the eyes of God."

Luckily, they now had several friends in their lives that encouraged their decision to back up and do things God's way plus a church where they blossomed in their faith.

Says Patricia, "We'd been together so long, we thought we had a handle on it. Our marriage really wouldn't have happened if it hadn't been for the church and God."

When asked to compare the differences they experienced in living together versus marriage, Patricia reports, "What the weight of marriage requires is far different than living together. We wanted to start a family and wanted to raise kids right. Having that commitment really drives living for each other, not for yourself.

"Before, we kinda had a lack of teamwork. We were just serving ourselves when we were first living together. We thought, 'We're adults, we're living alone, can stay out late as long as we want.'"

Patricia says in hindsight she looks back and says, "Man! What was I thinking? When we were younger we weren't even living together and were sexually active and having pregnancy scares so many times." They even went to a Planned Parenthood once thinking Patricia was pregnant. "We came so close to having to live with that burden," states Patricia.

For that and for the beautiful life and baby boy they now enjoy, Brandon and Patricia agree, "We've had it so much easier than so many people. We are so thankful for the people God brought. We are so incredibly blessed."

And what advice did Patricia have for her own younger sibling regarding sex and marriage? "I strongly say get married first then live together. We now understand we are wiser when we follow what God says. Sometimes we have to make all these mistakes to realize, 'Oh yeah. God was right.'"

> There are people out there who think, "This is fine. I'm in a committed relationship, we're being careful, etc. That's definitely better than going out and having one-nighters all the time, but it's still not God's best.
>
> WONDER-HUBBY MARK

CHAPTER 27

BOYS TO MEN

A couple years after writing my "What I'm looking for in a Husband" list, I was having a telephone conversation with a very cute guy from my crew of friends at church. We had been counselors at summer camp together where I had seen an amazing heart in him. Once, during a church service, I had glanced up during prayer and seen him bent over his drums (he was the worship band drummer) every line of his posture bent and broken before God. Something in me had melted. I loved his interest in all styles of music. I loved that he was kind yet obnoxious in a way that matched my own warped sense of humor. In fact, this guy named Mark was quickly becoming one of my best friends.

Suddenly, our phone conversation took a turn when he complained that even his family was giving him a hard time about his choices regarding sex and dating.

He quoted his family member as saying, "You know, the longer you wait, there's less chance the girl you choose will have waited too."

He went on talking, not even realizing how his words had just rocked my world. We weren't anything beyond friends, but it was so encouraging to hear that a guy like him even existed!

The fact Mark was in his twenties and still a virgin told me:

    a. He knew how to stick with commitment

    b. He strove to be in private what he professed in public

    c. He knew the meaning of self-control

    d. He wanted to please God even when it wasn't easy, fun, popular, or convenient

    e. He had deep desires and emotions but he could choose NOT to be ruled by them

Eureka! A real man!

A WORD TO GUYS

Here's the double-standard: Only the Girl needs to be concerned about practicing sexual self-control.

LIE!

Can STDs be spread by men?

YES.

Is a habit of promiscuity hard to break?

YES.

Can a guy bring sexual and emotional baggage into marriage?

Duh!

Who does the Bible say is to be the "Priest of the household?"

Right. The husband.

Who will be the living example to children of how a godly father and husband should live?

Right again. The man.

Who is a child's first example of God's love?

Daddy.

Where are the guys willing to stand up to the tidal wave of pornography, sexual addiction, selfishness, and basic wickedness to live full-out for God?

They're out there, but it may not seem like it, especially to the poor guys who are being fed such twisted images of how they should think and what they should strive for.

Guys, you're gonna feel like a salmon swimming upstream when you choose to put God first. But be encouraged by this. There's a breathtaking woman out there praying for you. There are godly men praying for this next generation of leaders. There are children who need to see a living, breathing example of God's kindness and love—in you—because they've had nothing but bad examples.

>A REAL man gets on his face before God.

>A REAL man is not a slave to physical desires.

> A REAL man knows how to repent, how to be humble, how to give grace because God has poured out grace (unearned favor) on him.
>
> A REAL man understands his job as a husband and father is to love his family the way Christ loved the church—laying down his life for them.

That takes guts.

The most macho thing I've ever seen? It's not a pro football player; not even a man decked out as a soldier, or John Wayne facing down the bad guy.

The manliest thing I've ever seen is a big, strapping guy cradling a newborn baby, holding that tiny child with his huge mitts as he looks with holy fear into wide, innocent eyes. It's a moment he discovers something precious that's worth living and dying for, something that makes his selfish ambitions go up in flames.

It's a moment his inner gladiator comes to life.
It's a moment that makes him desire to be a better man.
It's a moment when he grows up.

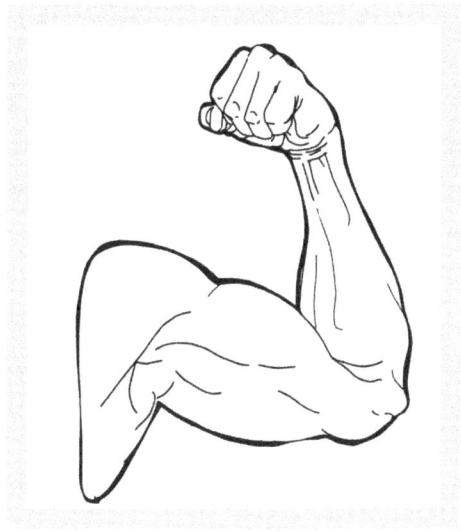

The world desperately needs more REAL men—men who aren't afraid to stand up for what's right, who are willing to play the fool if it's a choice between foolishness or faithlessness, men who put pleasing God above EV-E-RY-THING else.

Men like that change the world.

Many guys live a frustrated life because they're warriors at heart and it doesn't fit in polite society to strut with a sword at your side and blood-lust in your eyes. That's fine in a blockbuster movie but not in the real world.

Guys, the war these days is truly one of life and death—for now and for eternity. Too many of you have believed the lies and swallowed the poison that men are unneeded or masculinity is out of fashion. Don't believe it! Now more than ever we need you testosterone-driven warriors to protect our families. Aim that blood-lust toward the real war that's killing our families and stealing the hopes of future generations. *"We wrestle not against flesh and blood but against the principalities, powers and rulers of this present darkness." (Ephesians 6:12)*

The all-out war killing our families is on a spiritual, guerrilla-warfare level. Real men are needed who will lay down their selfish pursuits for their loved ones, who will pray over their homes, and seal the entrances each night with prayer with even more conviction than they lock the doors and windows. Every bit of the warrior in you is required to turn the tide that has separated fathers from their children and has removed men from the rightful place of protector/provider for their families.

I dare you to find a more constant, fierce battle than living as Christ lived in a world run amok. Talk about your nonconformist!

> Jesus made friends with society's outcasts.
>
> Jesus stood up to the powerful and prejudiced.
>
> Jesus loved though it cost him his reputation.
>
> Jesus put pleasing God ahead of ambition, family, and even his own life.

In today's context, Jesus would more likely resemble a tattooed Harley rider than a pastor in a three-piece suit. Outcasts like lepers, prostitutes, thieves, and the homeless felt comfortable with and accepted by Him.

His relationship with God kept getting Him in trouble. When people were healed and the demon-possessed were set free and the dead walked out of graves, He was accused of being full of the devil. The more good He did, the more He was hated.

Did He give up? Did He blame other people for his troubles and become bitter? Did He soften his message so people would like it? No.

You need a war? You need to buck convention? You need a fight against impossible odds? You want to follow a fearless leader? You want passion and fulfillment?

Study Jesus.

And when He says, "Follow me." Do it.

One more thing, guys. You too must choose your life's mate VERY carefully. Your wife can be a ball and chain around your neck or the wind beneath your wings. Read and reread Proverbs 31. Make your own list of what God tells you to look for in a wife and hold yourself to the highest possible standard. You are laying the foundation for your future home.

A woman who will be a strength to you and will remain faithful through life's many hard times will need talent in much more than sex appeal, hair, and make-up. As Proverbs 31 says, *"Charm is deceitful and beauty is vain but a woman who fears the Lord will be praised."*

God knows sex is important to you (don't deny it). Trust Him to bring the woman to you who can maintain your trust and admiration while she encourages the Godly warrior in you—and turns you on.

Great sex is about much more than physical allure. It's about a deep mental and spiritual bond, about freedom born of the highest regard for sacred vows, about intimacy with the person who encourages and protects your deepest vulnerability. The hidden treasure chambers of a couple united in God's love continue to open for a lifetime. That's why sex God's way truly gets better and better as the years go by.

That's what God wants you to have.

That's what the devil wants you to miss.

It's worth fighting for.

Ooh baby! Is it ever!

RECOMMENDED READING

For more on this topic, check out the excellent works of Ed Cole, author of *Maximized Manhood; Courage*, and several other titles aimed at the biblical definition of a real man's role: christianmensnetwork.com

CHAPTER 28
SINGLE AND INTIMATE

> "And when we begin to sort through all of the issues surrounding our sexuality, we quickly end up in the spiritual, because this is always about that. Sex. God. They're connected. And they can't be separated. Where the one is, you will always find the other."
> ROB BELL

I have a beautiful friend who would love to be married but God called her to minister in Hollywood, not a place known for churning out individuals committed to old-fashioned values. In the midst of a self-centered, morally-deficient society, she remains faithful, both physically and spiritually. She chooses to remain a virgin though she has been made to feel like a freak on several occasions. The sad thing is, although she moves in primarily Christian circles, she's often alone in her morality. One man who wanted to date her asked the question, "Are you a Christian who *will*, or a Christian who *won't*?"

It's a sad commentary on integrity when that question is necessary. We've homogenized the message of Christ so much the rest of the world can't even tell the difference between believers and non. No wonder our society continues to reject Christianity. Who wants to be numbered with the hypocrites?

I accept those judgments as a much-needed slap in the face. We as Christians love to point out the ills in society from rampant greed to bestiality but—*we are at fault*. Repeatedly in the Bible God says it's when *His people repent* that true revival will sweep the land—not when politicians repent or when race wars cease—but when those who claim to be followers of Christ start acting like it. (2 Chron. 7:14)

Jesus said we should live "in the world **but not of it.**" (John 17: 15-16) We tend to take that as an either/or proposition where one camp is so assimilated, they look just like the rest of our screwed-up society while the other end of the religious spectrum is so full of judgment, others are repelled by their lack of love and grace.

Let's make this clear. Your sexual experiences can be screwed up in such a way as to negatively affect your relationships with God and people BUT the deepest of intimacy with God and others is ***not dependent upon your having a sex life AT ALL.***

Sex is an avenue, a channel, by which God can share His love and open your heart, but He's a big God. He's got an endless supply of ways and means to reach His children.

In his book titled *Sex God*[20], Rob Bell says some of the most refreshingly intimate people he knows are single *and* completely fulfilled in their relationships with both God and people.

Your life is not on hold until you find your significant other. Neither are you handicapped in your service to God if you remain unmarried. Again, marriage and child rearing are great means to stretch yourself and deepen your relationship with God, but just ask the apostle Paul or Mother Teresa. Their fulfilling, exciting lives in Christ did not include sex—and they weren't missin' a thing!

Brittany is a beautiful young woman living a very full life who feels called to be single. But this can be frustrating. Says Brittany, "I'm very happily single. I don't know if I will someday be married, but it's not like a major desire of my heart." However, even good friends can sometimes misunderstand. "Somebody asked me, 'So are you like really, really single? Or do you have a side guy or whatever?' I said, 'I'm really single.'

Then my friend jumped in to ask the person we were chatting with, 'But do you know of anybody for this beautiful girl?' Kinda makes me furious."

Brittany has advice for young people who are going all-out for God. "Remember your identity is defined by God. I just wish that, single or not-single, people would realize that they're complete without another person. A person who comes along and keeps the pace, they should be a 'bonus' not a 'completion.'"

Brittany's wish for the way society views singleness? "When we have talks on relationships in the church—in society in general—there should be

---

20 *Sex God: Exploring the Endless Connections Between Sexuality and Spirituality* By Rob Bell

a singleness talk. People tend to think of singleness as a 'waiting period.' But it can be a lifestyle."

Brittany has had many friends who are guys, but over the years she has learned to ask God what He wants in these friendships. "As a Christian, there's a natural inclination of the Holy Spirit to want to help people." As a youth leader and mentor, Brittany has this advice for young women. "I tell my high school girls, 'you can save yourself from a lot of crap. Maybe God has placed someone in your life to pray for them—not pray for them to want you or to like you or to be your boyfriend." Plus, the addition of sex into relationships before marriage only leaves deeper wounds. "When I think about people who have broken my heart—because there have been people who have broken my heart—I think how awful it would be if sex had been involved."

Brittany's advice for how to approach any relationship: "They could very well be somebody else's spouse—they already belong to Christ, they're not yours. Even if you think you're going to marry them, they are still not yours… even if you're engaged."

Our true fulfillment is only available through God. In fact, one of the best ways to lay a healthy foundation for life is to commit to an extended season of "fasting" the opposite sex. No dates. No kissing. No striving to get their attention; just a focus on how to dig as deeply as possible into God's personality.

Whether your future holds a satisfying marriage or a lifetime of being single, God is still the love your heart seeks. The key is to commit your all to Him regardless of your life circumstances. Personally, I'd much prefer to be single than to be in a horrible marriage. But God is the key to both.

BETTER THAN SEX

I have an amazing marriage and have experienced mind-blowing, fulfilling sex with my best friend, the love of my life, and man of my dreams (all the same person BTW). But there are eternal moments I've experienced with God that have incomparably transcended sex.

How can I begin to describe the joy, tears, overflowing sense of fulfillment, and insatiable longing for more even when it seems this mortal body will explode with just one glance from my Creator? There's more beauty and mystery in one of God's thoughts toward me than a thousand lifetimes of marriage to the perfect man could ever supply.

It's happening again. I'm blubbering in the corner table of my favorite coffee shop as I wish so desperately for that day when I ditch this body and fly away home where the longing will finally be fulfilled. No bride ever longed for her wedding day with more passion and impatience, and yet these moments are like a gulp of air to enable me to survive in this hostile environment for one more day.

I love my husband and family with all my heart, and yet this connection to the lover of my soul is the one thing I couldn't live without.

Again, the complete connection with God is what we all seek. Nothing else will do. True fulfillment is not dependent on sex, which is a mere shadow of the blinding brilliance of losing yourself in your Maker.

Let your longing for a soul mate drive you toward the only One Who can truly fulfill you from the inside out. Whether single or married, that need can only be met by God.

CHAPTER 29
DEAR PARENTS

Why is it there are advertisements admonishing parents to talk to their kids about drugs, alcohol, and smoking but not about pre-marital sex?

Why is underage drinking or driving against the law, yet underage sex is a "personal choice?"

Why is it this personal choice can lead to a publicly-funded abortion?

Talking to teens can be difficult. As a parent you must choose to talk and keep on talking. If the connection with your teen is severed, spend time mending the rift. Maybe an apology on your part (or several) is in order. Find something you both enjoy and let the conversation flow. This may take time. Eventually, you may be able to open up about your own regrets and successes regarding sex. Talk about old loves that you thought were "forever" that didn't work out.

Maybe they'll roll their eyes and act allergic to the topic of sex. Good news—they'd probably have the same reaction to a discussion of drugs, nutrition, or modern fashion, so hang in there. If the only point-of-view regarding sex is from other teens trying desperately to act un-phased by life's mysteries, sex will be reduced in significance to just another thrill. Hopefully, as a parent who cares more for your child than you do for yourself, you've learned the true significance of sex—no less than a foundational event with potential ramifications that will resound through every other relationship and developmental decision for the rest of their lives.

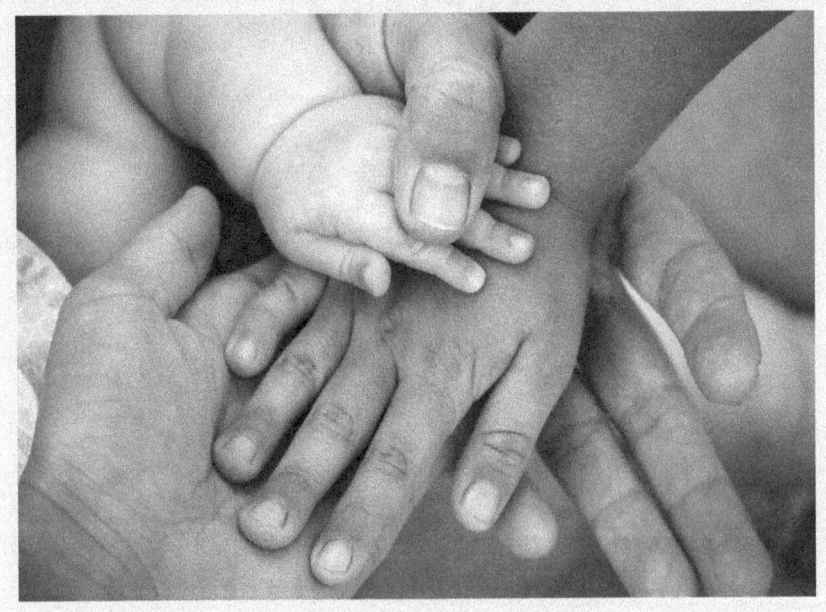

Don't be afraid to set loving boundaries. From that first time you warned your toddler of the danger of stepping out into the street or touching a hot stove, your job has been to forewarn and forearm. You wouldn't dream of sending them out into a blizzard without the proper protective clothing, so please don't let them wander into the minefield of sex without preparing them.

- **Have those "tough" discussions**
- **Set that curfew**
- **Meet their friends**
- **Interview their dates**
- **Know where they are and who they're with at all times.**

It's your job and, though they might act offended by your rules and involvement, at least they will know you care.

If your own sexual practices are dicey at best, *grow up*. How can you look your sixteen-year-old in the eye and encourage them to avoid sex until marriage when your live-in is in the next room? Don't allow yourself to be the chink in the armor or the breach in the wall of your kids' lives. What you do, *even if you think you're hiding it,* affects them. If you allow pornographic images in your home, don't be surprised if your kids are drawn to harmful practices. Set a high standard and stick with it. Put God first in your life. Maybe they'll roll their eyes about that too, but at least they can grudgingly admit you practice what you preach.

If you can't deny yourself bad habits for your own sake, *do it for your kids*. It's your God-ordained duty to protect and train them so, once again, **GROW UP.** You would never leave your kids prey to a sexual predator, so don't leave them vulnerable by throwing wide the door to sexual perversion.

Does it make a shiver of holy fear run down your spine to realize your kids are affected spiritually by your secret practices? Good. Now clean out those hidden little corners of your life for God's sake. Literally. Bring it out into the light, get counseling, pray with your spouse, confess, repent, and root out the stuff that would ruin not only your life but your kids' lives as well.

Over and over in the Bible when God speaks through His prophets about healing injustice and sinful practices in society, He will start with "turning the hearts of the fathers back to their children."[21] Can you imagine the fundamental shift in society's spiritual health if every parent who claims to be a believer got on their face before God and confessed their sins, repented, and started putting God's priorities into play in their homes? The children in those homes would have a foundation of secure love and wouldn't have such a gaping need to seek affection in promiscuity, thus the teen pregnancy rate would go down along with the abortion rate, the divorce rate, the number of kids raised without fathers and the number of juvenile crimes.

Follow this train of thought and the ramifications would resound in every facet clear down to unemployment and economics—unless we're speaking of the abortion industry, prison system, or organized crime that would implode due to the surge of strong nuclear families.

God understands the importance of foundations. If children have a strong root system—solid family, tons of love, people who cheer them on and model a moral life for them—they're like a tree that can withstand floods, fires and drought, or a castle that stands through a long siege.

Your personal purity practices (or screw ups) are stones in your children's foundation. Are you leaving them with a bunch of crap they're going to have to root out, or are your choices infusing them with strength?

---

21   Malachi 4:6; Luke 1:17

And if, despite your best efforts and prayers, your child pushes onto a destructive path, don't be afraid to halt their lives and stage a rescue. In the long-run, this will be the most loving thing you could do.

There is a real enemy longing to suck the life from the youth of today/ parents of tomorrow because Satan too understands foundations—how to sabotage them anyway. If your child had cancer you would take the steps necessary to eradicate it from their body. A spiritual cancer may require lovingly drastic means as well but, hopefully, the day will come when they will thank you.

DANIEL: AN EXAMPLE OF PARENTING DONE RIGHT

Several years ago Mark and I became acquainted with an awesome family raising four teenagers. Now, all four children from that family are happily married and maintain a loving relationship with Mom and Dad.

Their son Daniel was only sixteen when we met him, but already he was a confident, fun, moral young man. He was musically talented, handsome, and a basketball star to boot. He was the type of guy young ladies *and* their parents admired. Now Daniel and his wife Lisa are raising children of their own.

How in the world did Daniel make it as a virgin to his wedding night when Planned Parenthood would have us believe teens "*are* going to do it?" Furthermore, how did his parents manage to communicate their views in such a way that Daniel not only listened but also took their advice to heart?

Daniel says the most important factor in his own view of sex, and the fact that he entered marriage as a virgin, was his parents' instruction and attitude toward the subject. "They struck the right balance, not painting it as nasty and grotesque in general, because they were very clear that it could be a wonderful thing for married couples. They talked about sex respectfully, no crass remarks or casual jokes about sexuality."

In fact, Daniel's father had a serious man-to-man discussion about sex when Daniel was twelve and a real-life situation forced the issue. Says Daniel, "My hero, a high school basketball player at our school, got his girlfriend pregnant. I knew that wasn't a good thing, but I didn't know *how* someone gets pregnant. That was Dad's opportunity to have the man-talk with me."

Part of the proper balance Daniel's parents struck with their treatment of the topic of sex with Daniel and his sisters was the standard of morality as the loving parameters of a generous God. "I had a biblical grounding that created a healthy respect for the power of sex and what it, when handled wrongly, can do to people. I was taught that it was God's design and His gift to us, but it must be kept within the framework of marriage—only!"

Did his deep convictions regarding sex make it easy to remain a virgin until his wedding night? Not at all. Daniel says he had to face his share of temptations even in the relatively sheltered atmosphere of a private Christian high school and college. In fact, he tells the story of a high school graduation celebration when two beautiful girls made aggressive suggestions regarding how the three of them could make use of the snack table's strawberries and whipped cream. He refused their advances but admits he was sorely tempted. "Of course, they had to be gorgeous," Daniel notes with sarcasm. "The Bible says to flee, so I did."

Even in college, Daniel stayed true to those standards and his parents' instruction. "I still had desires, but I truly believed entering marriage as a virgin was the best way."

Did this treatment of sex stunt Daniel's social or even sexual development? Not in the least. Daniel had no shortage of friends, exciting opportunities, or even girlfriends. He encourages young people—high school and young adult—to take advantage of the extra time and energy that would normally be invested in sexual relationships and redirect it toward relationship with God, great friendships, sports, leisure, studies, and music. "This is your time to invest in those things and they'll pay off for you down the line."

Daniel says the casual approach to sex pushed by popular media is brutally deceptive. "Sex is not what culture (TV, Hollywood, magazine covers, etc.) paints it to be," says Daniel. The lie that sex is just fun and it doesn't matter who you have sex with or that there will be no consequences to those choices is just that; a lie.

"God designed a husband and wife to enjoy sex. To those who think sex can be enjoyed on one's own terms, I'd say: sexual climax is not great enough to throw your life away. It's not worth losing your health, sanity, and soul."

And now, as a happily married husband and father, Daniel says he is so grateful he chose to approach sex from a biblical point-of-view. "Let's be honest—sexual climax, technically speaking, is a great feeling at any time and can, realistically, be achieved with anyone," Daniel states. "But it can only be *great*, in the truest, long-term sense of the word, when it is enjoyed in accordance with God's ways."

After several years of married life, Daniel has this perspective about saving sex for marriage. "It saves you from unnecessary jealousy and mental torment. Now, having been intimate with Lisa for so long, I couldn't imagine if, while we were being intimate (or anytime for that matter!) I was wondering about other guys she had been with and wondering if she enjoyed them more, etc. That would crush me and it would hinder intimacy. Learning how to be intimate is hard enough without that drama, but I imagine it'd be even harder if there were other, previous partners."

Daniel says he has never regretted the sexual opportunities he bypassed. "Pay it forward, people. Have something to look forward to."[22]

---

22   Daniel Grothe is an author and pastor ministering in Colorado. Check out his book: *Chasing Wisdom: The Lifelong Pursuit of Living Well*

CHAPTER 30

A SEX REVOLUTION!

In respectable relationships of yesteryear, the young man had a pretty good idea he had found a candidate for a wife before he ever made his intentions known. He had the guts to approach the young lady's dad and ask permission to court her before he came to call. When he did, they were chaperoned while they became better acquainted, their interactions under the watchful, protective eye of Mom and Dad. It wasn't just the young man and woman whose opinion mattered. The family also had a vote and their approval was crucial, generally referred to as *giving their blessing* to the proposed union before the young man popped the question.

How much pain could be avoided if we returned to a more old-fashioned dating approach. The fellow "comes to court" but the couple is not allowed situations that would even appear compromising. That way, if the two young people realize their relationship is not suitable for the long haul, the deep emotional scars due to the baring of body and soul to someone who exits your life never happens.

Is it any wonder our ability to maintain satisfying relationships has dwindled as our respect for the act of sex has declined?

It is possible to do things God's way, preserving not only your own sexual integrity but protecting the hearts of those you "court." Are you willing to be radical, a sexual maverick who values yourself and others enough to take God at His word?

In 2 Chronicles, the Bible says the eyes of the Lord rove over the earth seeking someone who is fully committed to Him. [23] Dare to be the one, even if you feel alone in your efforts, who will take God at His word, stick to what's right against all odds, and build a life that shines like a lighthouse in the storm of relational devastation.

No matter where you are, no matter what you've done, your future can be a testament of God's love, redemption, and sexual resurrection. Press in to Him and hang on tight because nothing gets God's attention more quickly than simple, childlike faith to take Him at His word and live accordingly.

A true sexual revolution God's way will get to the marrow of the matter, to the heart of our yearning to connect with a God of transforming power.

The beauty is, this generation is hungry. They're ready for change.

It's time for revolution. It's time for a radical return to sexual responsibility and wholesome priorities. It's time to point people to the One who became a curse for us so we can be healed.

---

[23] 2 Chron. 16:9 "For the eyes of the Lord run to and fro throughout the whole earth, to show Himself strong on behalf of those whose heart is loyal to Him."

Like John the Baptist said, "He must increase, I must decrease."[24] Then the world will see something worth living and dying for.

They will see something BETTER THAN sex and they'll want it. They'll want it *bad*.

They'll want it so much, in fact, they'll realize their thirst is for God. And God will answer their heart's cry, healing hearts, minds, and bodies and reminding the frozen chosen in our churches that we serve a God of POWER.

It's sexual revolution God's way—from the inside out—bringing health and freedom to the hidden places of the heart until it bubbles to the surface like a deep, pure mountain spring.

Then sex slavery would go belly-up, the abortion industry would fail, divorce attorneys' phones would stop ringing, and children would enjoy a stable home where their parents are crazy in love with God and crazy in love with each other. That's what "God healing our land" would look like.

I'm crazy enough to dream of, repent for, stay on my knees for, *be a fool for* that revolution.

Join me.

---

24   John 3:30 "He must increase. I must decrease."

QUICK REFERENCE GUIDE

1. Make sure God is your foundation and source
    a. What do you think about the most?
    b. What do you talk about the most?
    c. What controls your emotions?
2. Make a Dream List for your future mate—Top of the list: God is FIRST
3. Keep that list handy to decide who's "dateable"
4. Set some parameters:
    a. Watch how you dress
    b. Have them meet the family
    c. Set a curfew
    d. Avoid alcohol and other "numbing" influences
5. Are you an exhibitionist?
6. Root out your weaknesses
7. If you've screwed up, run to God.
8. Infatuation or True Love? Know the difference.
9. Draw the line:
    a. Kissing is far enough
    b. Bathing suit zone is off-limits
    c. Clothes stay ON
10. Stay Alert! Humility is your best defense
11. God is your source of healing
12. God is the true intimacy we all seek

RECOMMENDED RESOURCES

And the Bride Wore White—Dannah Gresh

Courage—Dr. Edwin Cole

Maximized Manhood—Dr. Edwin Cole

Do Hard Things: A Teenage Rebellion Against Low Expectations—Alex and Brett Harris

Family Rules—Positive Parenting With a Plan by Dr. Matthew Johnson

therebelution.com —a forum for teens rebelling against low expectations

Love and Fidelity Organization—a campus support group: Building the next generation of leaders for marriage, family, and sexual integrity.

Positivelywaiting.com Positively Waiting! The Art of Sexual Self-Control

Sex God: Exploring the Endless Connections Between Sexuality and Spirituality by Rob Bell

ACKNOWLEDGEMENTS

The process of writing *Great Love for Life* has been long, involved and enlightening. I started with a simple premise: "What do I want my own kids to understand about their sexual choices?" But to expand my own knowledge base and gain a wider view, the ATEAM was an indispensable experience. Through them, I had the amazing opportunity to stand before many high school classes full of teens, look in those eyes and push past fear to share the most loving message about their worth.

Therefore, I am forever indebted to Bob Shatto, founder of ATEAM, and Mark Fortier, my partner in these talks. Also, Karen Kropf of Positively Waiting, what a dynamo you are. Thank you for giving me such a clear view of God's redemption through your transparent sharing of your story and your tenacity in the face of opposition.

To the many who opened their lives to share in the pages of this book and even in recorded videos (available on Youtube for further study) thank you so much for trusting me.

Huge kudos to the amazing Yvonne Parks of PearCreative.ca for your cover art & formatting wizardry. Dang, girl, you make me look good!

To my kids Micah, McKenna, Sky and Madeline, many thanks for opening my heart to love so deeply that, prude that I am, I would delve into this touchy subject. I am so proud of the amazing young adults you are. I pray constantly for your life mates. What lucky people they will be.

To my hubby Mark, life partner and soul mate, thank you for joining me on this journey. Thank you for being unashamedly clueless and hilarious on our first night of marriage. (NLV!) And thank you for continuing to live out what true love looks like every day of our lives together.

To the prayer warriors and heart friends who cheered me on and listened to my rants, bless you for your support and unending patience.

To Mom and Dad, I'll always miss you until I join you in Heaven. Thank you for showing me that love stays, especially when life is hard.

Much gratitude to Real Life Church, our church home for lo these many years!

And lastly, my debt of gratitude to the number one aim and love and Lord of my life, Holy Papa God, is never ending. You show up every day, every moment of joy and pain. Your compassion and wisdom and grace and mindboggling love is my everything.

For orders or to contact Chana regarding speaking engagements, Book Clubs, or online group meetings go to:

chanakeefer@icloud.com
Website: chanakeefer.com
Facebook: fb.com/chanakeeferauthor
Instagram: @Chana Keefer
YouTube: Chana Keefer

Meet some of the amazing folks featured in
GLFL: Great Love for Life: The Interviews

Chana's books are also available on:
Amazon
Barnes & Noble
Smashwords
Kobo

What is the power of ONE LIFE fully placed in God's hands? Chana's #1 Bestselling books explore some fascinating possibilities. From epic Inspirational Fiction to empowering non-fiction, one person, standing firm in faith, has the power to rock the world. Delve into these books, alone or with a group. Let them inspire you toward your own epic life.

THE FALL
(THE RAPHA CHRONICLES #1)

TOP-RATED & #1 AMAZON BESTSELLER IN SCIENCE FICTION, MESSIANIC JUDAISM, & OLD TESTAMENT!

Rapha, once Lucifer's best friend, had a front-row seat for every crucial moment that shaped the world in which we live. This faithful angel wants to tell you his story. But beware. This is not a journey for the faint-of-heart. Ahead there be giants—plus demons, centaurs, mermaids, demi-gods and war that extends from the beginning of time. In the tradition of J.R.R. Tolkien, C.S. Lewis and Frank Peretti, The Fall: (Rapha Chronicles, Book 1) melds cutting-edge Inspirational Science Fiction, Fantasy, Epic Adventure, and Mythology.

Includes a guide for group or individual study.

RAVES FOR
THE FALL: RAPHA CHRONICLES, BOOK 1

"A massive, visual spectacle... Epic does not begin to cover it."

"A challenging, beyond-epic fictional story that screams "Truth!" with razor-sharp metaphors about the nature of Good and Evil..."

"Allow this book to break your heart and open you up to God's boundless love!"

"Fantastically rich in every aspect!"

"Thank you for connecting my hurting soul to the Healer of ALL."

"I can easily see this becoming a movie on the scale of *Lord of the Rings*."

"The beginning of a new era in Christian fantasy."

THE ONE NIGHT WITH A ROCK STAR SERIES

ONE NIGHT WITH A ROCK STAR: COMPLETE 2-BOOK SERIES (Book 1 & Part Deux)

#1 Amazon Inspirational Hot New Release;
#1 in 10 Amazon categories

When Esther was a young teen with frizzy hair and too-skinny legs, Sky's music soothed her through awkwardness and pain. During the Glam-Rock 80s, Esther is a college journalism student and fledgling print model. One chance meeting with her superstar crush rocks both their worlds.

Will Esther's deep roots in family and faith keep her feet on the ground when a tornado named Sky blows her world apart?

One Night With a Rock Star is a rich, satisfying journey filled with multi-dimensional, lovable characters and a tale that will carve itself onto your soul.

RAVES FOR ONE NIGHT WITH A ROCK STAR

"Drew me in like a hot steaming coffee on an icy winter's day."

"My new favorite book!"

"Great message for singles!"

"I felt like I was living the story… I recommended (*Rock Star*) to my teenage daughter so she can find solace in her personal convictions."

"Why can I not give this more stars!
Never in my life have I loved a book this much!"

"Among my top five favorites of all time!"

"As captivating as *Twilight* with the added bonus of God."

ANNABELLE: A GHOSTLY TEXAS TALE

#1 Hot New Family Classic Release

A once-grand house, neglected and abused. A young family on the brink of meltdown.

Rumors of a resident ghost? That's the least of their problems.

When Jansen and Kate Walden move from the West Coast to small town Texas, they hope a fresh start will help their shredded family heal. But adding huge renovation bills and unexpected hardships only pushes them closer to tragedy.

In their darkest moments, light and hope come from a very surprising source. But is there enough magic left in the old Pedigo Manor to keep Jansen & Kate from making tragic mistakes?

Need a captivating story that highlights and gives hope for the struggles facing modern families? Answers for life's tough questions? Faith to draw near to God when everything hits the fan? *Annabelle: A Ghostly Texas Tale* is just what the doctor ordered and is the perfect conversation catalyst for today's war-weary families.

RAVES FOR ANNABELLE

"Perfect read for a winter's night, cozy by the fireplace... and in the dark!"

"What a powerful and anointed story. I'm crying happy tears."

"These characters will live on in my head and heart."

STUDY GUIDE INCLUDED FOR INDIVIDUAL OR GROUP USE.

Discussion topics: Anger; Bullying; Pornography; Sexual Abuse; Sexual Responsibility; Infidelity; Addiction; Shame.

Appropriate for ages 12 & up.

SERVANT OF THE KING:
MEMOIR OF MODERN APOSTLE KEMPER CRABB

11 MILLION SALVATIONS.
1,800 CHURCHES.
400 ORPHANAGES.
17 RESURRECTIONS.
3-TIME NOBEL PEACE PRIZE NOMINEE. (Now 5-time)

From the palaces of kings, to the slums of India, and to the belly of dungeon-like prisons, Kemper Crabb spreads salvation, love, and alleviation of suffering. It started with one suffering child. Armed Gurkhas would not let Kemper near the child for fear he would "alter Karma." The child died—frightened, alone, and unloved. Kemper cried out to God, "Why do You allow such suffering?" God answered

Kemper with a vision of the child sitting on Jesus' knee. But He also gave the heartbroken missionary much more: a vision of how to relieve the spiritual and physical suffering of millions.

Included: Kemper's Spiritual Warfare Training Handbook

ENDORSEMENTS

"Kemper is very, very unique. He set out to help children and has to deal with far darker things of the black market and kids dying. Some have waited a lifetime to hear what Kemper Crabb is saying. His spiritual perspective of what is going on worldwide challenges us to believe in the power of Christ."

Brett Rogers
University of Texas College Director for Young Life Ministries

"I've known Kemper Crabb for more than 70 years. Mother Teresa nominated him for the Nobel Peace Prize and he's received the Distinguished Alumni Achievement Award from Delta Tau Delta. Kemper is doing a ton of good for others for eternity."

Charles Mallery,
Retired Exxon/Mobile Independent Consultant
& lifelong witness of Kemper Crabb s life

"This is a must read if you are looking for something to stretch your faith to realize nothing is impossible for God."

Bill Rieser
Celebrate Recovery Pastor at Real Life Church,
Evangelist, & Author of *Vertical Leap.*

READER REVIEWS

"As a Christian wife, mother, and seminary student, I have come to appreciate a good book when one crosses my path. This book is certainly at the top of that list."

"Reading Kemper's story is like reading a chapter out of the bible. Miracles, Angel encounters, healing and God's sovereign power in action!"

"I love to read but I read slowly so the book really has to keep my attention for me to take the time to read it! The story of Kemper Crabb is riveting!"

"Living in the modern world, two foundational truths often escape us: Evil is real, and God is bigger. Servant of the King illustrates, from a first-hand perspective, both of these truths."

"A must read for the believer and the nonbeliever as well. What happens on the mission trips that Kemper takes, and those of us who are honored enough to accompany, is truly miraculous. We are honored to have such a man who believes that 'we can do what Jesus did because it says so right in the Bible.' (John 14:12) A well-written, fascinating story!"

"Not only is it an easy read, but the stories of this Man's life are absolutely incredible. The words in this book have changed me and challenged me to take my life to a new level. It's an EXCELLENT read!"

"Extremely well-written book. Kemper is a modern-day Paul. Constantly probing the mysteries of Christ! A must read."

"Servant of the King is a must read for every believer, especially if you think that the Age of Miracles may have come to an end."

Excerpt from Servant of the King: Memoir of Modern Apostle Kemper Crabb

The man drew no attention to himself in the crowd filing toward the waiting airplane.

Clothed in blue jeans and collared shirt, no one would think he had been imprisoned multiple times, held hundreds of dying children in his arms, or worked side-by-side with Mother Teresa.

He was simply an aging man with a kind smile and alert expression. He was overlooked by all—except the one who stood at the door of the terminal, another who was ignored by the crowd—because no one else could see him.

The messenger's words were concise:

"Heavenly servant, it is time to tell your story."

For orders or to contact Chana regarding speaking engagements, Book Clubs, or online group meetings go to:

chanakeefer@icloud.com
Facebook: Chana Keefer, Author
Instagram: Chana Keefer
Website: chanakeefer.com
Youtube: Chana Keefer

Thank you for reading *Great Love For Life*. I hope it brought you encouragement and joy like it did for me to write it.

Can I give you a free gift to say thanks?

Go to my website, <u>chanakeefer.com</u>, and enter the code **GREATLOVE** for a super-special gift from my heart to yours.

Again, thank you so much!